# Lead Me— I Dare You!

## Managing Resistance to School Change

**Sherrel Bergmann**
**Judith Brough**

EYE ON EDUCATION
6 DEPOT WAY WEST, SUITE 106
LARCHMONT, NY 10538
(914) 833–0551
(914) 833–0761 fax
www.eyeoneducation.com

**Library of Congress Cataloging-in-Publication Data**

Bergmann, Sherrel.
Lead me, I dare you! : managing resistance to school change / Sherrel
Bergmann, Judith Brough.
    p. cm.
    ISBN 1-59667-044-4
    1. Educational leadership. 2. School management and organization. 3.
Conflict management. 4. Interpersonal relations. I. Brough, Judith
Allen.
    II. Title.
LB2805.B46 2007
371.2—dc22

                                        2006102441

10 9 8 7 6 5 4 3 2 1

Editorial and production services provided by
Freelance Editorial Services
52 Oakwood Blvd.
Poughkeepsie, NY 12603-4112

## *Also Available from* EYE ON EDUCATION

**Teach Me – I Dare You!**
Judith Brough, Sherrel Bergmann, and Larry Holt

**What Great Principals Do *Differently*:**
**15 Things That Matter Most**
Todd Whitaker

**What Successful Principals Do!**
**169 Tips for Principals**
Franzy Fleck

**Creating the High Schools of Our Choice**
Tom Westerberg

**Improving Your School One Week at a Time:**
**Building the Foundation for Professional Teaching & Learning**
Jeffrey Zoul

**Effective Schooling for English Language Learners:**
**What Elementary Principals Should Know and Do**
Patricia Smiley and Trudy Salsberry

**Lead With Me: A Principal's Guide to Teacher Leadership**
Gayle Moller and Anita Pankake

**The Instructional Leader's Guide**
**to Informal Classroom Observations**
Sally J. Zepeda

**Coaching and Mentoring**
**First Year and Student Teachers, Second Edition**
India Podsen and Vicki Denmark

**Countdown to the Principalship:**
**A Resource Guide for Beginning Principals**
O'Rourke, Provenzano, Bellamy, and Ballek

**Improving Your Elementary School:**
**Ten Aligned Steps for Administrators, Teams, Teachers,**
**Families and Students**
Leslie Walker Wilson

**Smart, Fast, Efficient:**
**The New Principals' Guide to Success**
Leanna Stohr Isaacson

# Acknowledgments

The inspiration for this book came from the hundreds of excellent administrators and school leaders that we have met over the past twenty five years. As a part of the quest for excellence in their schools, those leaders did whatever was necessary to involve everyone in the change process. We selected a few that we knew had been effective change agents in a variety of settings and asked them for their input. Each of them had unique skills in dealing with resistance. The heart of this book is in their interviews and success stories. For their dedication, effort, persistence, skill, success, and willingness to share, we thank Bill Burke, Tom Gunning, John Haschak, Linda Holdorf, Al Moyer, Marion Payne, Bess Scott, and Ron Williamson. They represent leadership at its best.

# Table of Contents

◆ v

# Introduction

# Lead Me — I Dare You! Managing Resistance to School Change

Every politician, religious leader, business leader, and school leader has met them. Their resistance to change and their reluctance to be involved disrupt the culture and progress of any organization. In some cases, their reluctance is based on a history of ineffective leadership. In others, it is a personal problem or perspective that makes them reluctant. There are many variables that affect their behavior. Whatever the reason, they are easy to spot and challenging to deal with.

The chapters in this book offer concrete strategies, research, and success stories for dealing with resistance and reluctant followers. Underlying the premise that there are both leaders and followers in every group, there is an assumption that everyone can and should both lead and follow. Helping followers develop leadership skills can only strengthen an organization.

This book, like its predecessor, *Teach Me—I Dare You*, is about people who dare others to learn, grow, participate, help, or make a difference. Though the first book was about adolescents, this one is about all age groups, but the particular focus is on adults in organizations, especially schools. These are adults who teach, mentor, coach, or work with others and refuse to change. They are also adults who influence the lives of children and adolescents by their very nature and modeling. They may have a better idea about how to solve a problem, but they do not know how to communicate it.

They enter meetings with the daily paper, sit in the back row, and make challenging remarks whenever the leader begins the meetings. They refuse to volunteer for any projects that might change their daily routine. Their allegiance is to something other than their job or their colleagues. They have good ideas, but they refuse to share them. They may be male or female, of any age, any level of education, and any place in the world. They refuse to vote, participate, get involved, or alter their routine. They may try subversively to start another group and get rid of the leader.

This book was inspired by observations and interactions with leaders who were dared to lead an organization to change—and took the dare. None of the leaders in this book had special training in how to deal with those who dared them, but they all instinctively knew what to do. All of them were just typical leaders in typical situations. But their leadership skills were the same in almost every success story. They were all interviewed separately, yet they all agreed on the strategies that need to be used.

Although the consequences of reluctant followership may be different in business, politics, and school, the characteristics of reluctant or resistant followers are the same.

Much of our history has been built by resistant followers, but it has been the leadership within the ranks of the followers who have brought large groups of people forward. Disagreement with leadership is not necessarily bad for an organization. Power hungry, abusive, or ineffective leaders have made changes in organizations, but it has rarely been for the universal good. They have created reluctant followers.

Chapter 1 looks at the development of leadership and followership attitudes, types of followers, and the levels of resistance that a leader can use to measure the degree of resistance in a group. The chapter closes with the success story of a leader who made significant changes in several school districts and is still training new leaders.

Chapter 2 describes the characteristics of reluctant followers, such as Ben There and his buddy, Don That, as well as 10 reasons why school personnel don't follow a leader. This chapter includes a powerful success story of a leader who used the vision and action planning process to turn around an extremely static faculty who feared change. A teacher leader who has been a part of several significant changes offers her perspective on leadership and change.

Chapter 3 provides an in-depth look at how leaders can assess the personality types and talents of reluctant followers and use that information to help a staff move forward. In addition, this chapter shows how emotional intelligence; multiple intelligences; and cultural, racial, and gender differences affect a person's willingness to participate in the change process. Success stories from a district administrator are shared.

Chapter 4 defines the characteristics of effective leaders and explains how culture influences leadership. Skills for assessing your own leadership style and development are offered. Leaders must analyze the culture of their school or organization and determine the degree of resistance they face. This can be done by becoming a reflective professional. Two success stories about leaders who helped to change many schools are offered.

Chapter 5 offers strategies for motivating reluctant followers and suggests using the Professional Learning Community approach. The use of vision, values, and celebrations with reluctant followers is also discussed. A success story of an elementary principal with a unique model of change is provided.

Chapter 6 provides specific strategies for helping reluctant followers found in both the literature and the interviews. It provides communication skills for taking the dare and helping people feel as if they are a part of the organization. It, too, provides a success story of a principal who made many changes and turned around several highly reluctant teachers with his communication skills.

Chapter 7 provides skills and ideas for helping community members, parents, teams, and students become leaders in a school. Promoting positive following and leading should be the goal of any school administrator. Building a pool of people who can lead and help the organization move forward is an essential skill for any leader. Student leadership can be developed through special projects and programs provided by the school.

This chapter also focuses on the importance of teaming and staff development as long-range strategies for reducing the number of reluctant followers. Special resources are offered for developing student and parent leadership in the school. A success story from a district administrator offers sound advice for involving parents and the community in the change process.

Chapter 8 provides a staff development exercise called "Who Killed Learning?" that can be used by leaders to get the faculty to look at teaching styles, attitudes, and willingness to change in a humorous way. The characters in the exercise are all reluctant followers who have hampered the change process in a school. The characters in this exercise were submitted to the authors by school leaders.

This book is not intended to promote any one person or idea; rather, it is a compilation of best practices in leading for school change that we have researched and observed. There are countless other leaders in schools who are being challenged by and challenging reluctant followers every day. Their struggles to bring along reluctant followers would fill a separate volume. We salute their efforts and hope the ideas presented in this book can help those who struggle with reluctant followers to bring about the changes that are needed for the benefit of their students.

# 1

# Defining the Degree of Followership

Penny Principal was hired because the retiring superintendent was tired of hearing parents and teachers complain that the high school was out of control. Teachers complained about the lack of decision making in the building. In her interview, she seemed like the perfect leader for the building. Her goals were to raise test scores and to implement the state curriculum. Her goals were sound, but her methods created chaos.

Penny Principal was "in charge" of her building. She worked very hard to develop her authoritarian style and did not let anyone forget that she made all the decisions. She only believed in self-empowerment and did not even allow teachers to talk at faculty meetings. She ran her building like a military command center, with no interaction between herself and anyone else. She was totally unapproachable to students and staff and gave weekly calendars of items that must be accomplished. All lesson plans were subject to careful scrutiny and criticism. Parents avoided the school as much as possible. She followed every state mandate to the letter and vowed never to let flexibility enter her building. She ruled by fear and intimidation and wondered, after the first year, why the scores had gone down and teachers were asking for transfers. She was the perfect example of how to lose support for the administration. Teachers whispered to each other in the parking lot, "Be careful what you ask for in a leader, you might get it."

In the next county, a new leader had been hired for the local elementary school. In only six weeks, his school was filled with reluctant followers.

Dr. Daily Decree had a list of credentials that amazed the school board. He was a specialist in several content areas, a constant participant in conferences and workshops, and a bandwagon hopper. The only skill he lacked was the ability to work with people. Every week, he decreed some change in his elementary school. He would go off to a conference, gather some new ideas, and tell his staff to start doing them. His most famous flop was the magic circle. With proper staff development, the magic circle is a great way for students to share ideas and concerns. However, this school leader did not believe staff development was necessary. On Monday morning, he announced that every classroom that day would have a magic circle for 15 minutes. Unfortunately, he had failed to tell his teachers what this was, so speculation and frustration were high among the staff members. Some wondered whether it was an assembly, others thought that it might have something to do with the lighting, and most just dismissed it as another one of his strange ideas. No one did anything different, but most waited to see whether anything would happen in their classrooms. His leadership style and lack of direction created an entire community of fearful resistant followers.

Both of these leaders had personal flaws that kept them and their schools from achieving. Their styles caused such dissension in their buildings that the teachers became distrustful of anyone holding a leadership position. The concept of the reluctant follower is not new to schools or human history. It is human nature to be skeptical of change. Every leader faces reluctance on the part of his or her followers and reluctant followers can become leaders. Leaders can learn how to deal with reluctant followers by studying those who have been both successful and unsuccessful.

Throughout history, kings and queens who ruled by birthright faced whole countries of reluctant followers and used many means to silence or remove them. Some were sent from the country, whereas others were tortured and even lost their heads. Resistance to leadership took the form of wars, underground movements, and civil disobedience. Some of the greatest leaders of all time were quietly sabotaged by reluctant followers. Others, such as Abraham Lincoln, were openly attacked by newspapers and public speakers.

Leaders are often faced with reluctant followers because of ideals, ideas, or personal grievances. Political and religious leaders are especially vulnerable to the spoken and written actions of those who disagree with their vision and policies. However, we know from history that reluctance to follow is not necessarily a negative trait.

Our nation was founded by reluctant followers who used subversive resistance and then active resistance to dump the tea in Boston Harbor and then start the Revolutionary War against the leadership of England. Those followers became the leaders of our new country and fostered new ideas about the effectiveness of dissent. Later, dissent against leadership and personal power fueled the civil rights and women's movements, proving that not all followers who dare leaders are negative influences. Some followers who resist leadership actually have better ideas, better problem-solving skills, and a set of universal values that are larger than a single issue.

Great leaders often have to swim against the current of popular opinion. When the number of reluctant followers becomes larger than the number of supporters, leaders search for a core of supporters who have a clear idea of the mission and goals of the organization. They must identify the degree of dissent, the purpose of dissent, and the level of commitment to dissent. Great leaders see their constituents as sharing a universal view of the purpose and goals of the organization. They use that core of support to help them sway reluctant followers. Kids call this "peer pressure." Leaders fail because they are unable to find a core of support for their universal ideas or ideals. They fail to analyze the culture in which they are functioning and fail to understand those who refuse to follow. Other leaders fail because they do not model the changes they want to see in others. As Gandhi said, "Be the change you want to see in the world." Leaders cannot say one thing and do something else. Historically, leaders have been removed from their leadership position when they could not muster a majority of followers.

When leaders are appointed for some reason other than their skills and knowledge, they run a higher risk of having reluctant supporters. Perhaps one of the most helpful research projects of the past decade looked at the leadership of great companies. In identifying the variables that made for successful leaders, the researchers found that "good to great leaders seem to have come from Mars. Self-effacing, quiet, reserved, even shy—these leaders area paradoxical blend of person humility and professional will. They are more like Lincoln and Socrates than Patton and Caesar" (Collins, 2001, p. 13). In addition, they found that great leaders got the right people on the bus, the wrong people off the bus, and the right people in the right seats—and then "they figured out where to drive it" (p. 13). These words of wisdom from successful businesses can be directly applied to leadership in schools and the quest to bring along reluctant followers.

## Leadership and Followership Begin at an Early Age

Leadership and followership are observable when children play. Watch an elementary school recess and look at who decides what will be done during free time. The classic children's game "Follow the Leader" requires a leader who is either self-selected, appointed by the group, appointed by an adult, or next in line when taking turns. Usually, children take turns, and everyone gets to practice leading and following. The concept is simple: One child leads the group in a task, and the rest of the group tries to do the same task. However, there are some children who never want to be the leader and some who always want to dominate. Children who are more verbal tend to make decisions for others. Some follow but try to sabotage the efforts of the group.

As children become adolescents, the concept of the game is the same, but the leaders emerge in athletics, academics, student government, church groups, and street gangs. Again, they are selected, elected, appointed, or anointed, either by themselves or by the group. Though there may be reluctant followers, they usually drop out rather than speak out in the group. The common element is that a group is attempting to achieve a common goal and someone is in charge of moving them toward that goal. Leadership among adolescents may be the most tenuous of all, as group loyalties change so frequently. Adolescents can develop positive leadership skills when they are provided with opportunities through the school and the community.

Adults are quick to notice leadership characteristics in adolescents that are both positive and negative. They may also notice those adolescents who participate in life only as followers. The leaders and followers of childhood eventually end up as members of a community in which their actions can make a significant difference in the lives of others. That community may be a school, a business, a religious group, a government, or an organization with a common mission. Adults continue to play Follow the Leader, but the tasks are more difficult, and the consequences of not following are more complex.

Whether schools lead society or follow society is a frequent topic of debate among scholars and school leaders. The extent to which a business is socially responsible as part of its profit making is a common topic in board meetings and the news media. Whether religious groups can maintain their followers and remain true to their philosophy is what religious leaders ponder. Whether a government is leading a country or culture in the "right direction" is determined by elections and wars. In the end, it is all about common goals, continuous progress, how a leader obtains leadership, how much the leader is willing to share power, and the attitudes of the followers.

Leaders need followers in order to achieve the goals of the organization. With increasing access to information about the organization, whether it is a school, business, or religious group, followers have become more empowered and well informed. Most school leaders realize that creating a highly qualified group of followers is critical to increasing the performance of students.

What, then, are the essential qualities of effective followers? According to research by Robert E. Kelley (1988),

- They are able to set their own goals and decide what role to play within the organization.

- They are committed to a purpose beyond themselves.

- They work to improve their own skills and strive to do their best.
- They are honest, credible, and courageous. They are also self-reliant, enthusiastic, and intelligent.

Being truthful to leaders is essential in the school setting, where information about students is readily shared. Good leaders respect followers who speak up and share their ideas. Reluctant followers who withhold information and refuse to give honest opinions are inclined to hide information that might make them or their teaching look bad. They tend to be critical, cynical, apathetic, and alienated. They focus on what can go wrong rather than what is possible (Bjugstad, Thach, Thompson, & Morris, 2006, p. 308).

Many reluctant followers dwell on problems rather than seek solutions. They may create a culture of low morale and regression rather than one of progress.

## Four Types of Followers

Kelley (1988) defines four types of followers:

1. Alienated followers who are capable but cynical.
2. Conformist followers who are the "yes" people of the organization. They do their jobs and follow orders.
3. Passive followers who require constant direction and let the leader do the thinking for them.
4. Exemplary followers who are independent, innovative, and willing to question the leadership. They work well with others and represent the organization in a positive and consistent manner.

A main goal of leadership is to get reluctant followers to take an active role in the progress of the organization and thus take ownership of the ongoing success. In schools, teachers who are exemplary followers see the success of their students as the outcome of the success of the organization.

In every group in which there are leaders, there will be followers who are skeptical about the leadership and who say, verbally or nonverbally, "Lead me—I dare you." Those who take the dare and succeed have a specific set of skills that they use. How they make it and why they make it are the essential questions discussed in this book. Studies of successful leaders, group dynamics, and followership have given a number of strategies that leaders can use to answer the dare. Schools and classrooms may house the best examples of skeptics who dare their leaders. Students who ask why they have to learn something and teachers who ask why they have to teach something are daily reminders of the dare for school leaders. Consider the following actions of a new high school principal.

Bob had been appointed the new principal over the summer. Two teachers had been invited to join the final selection process, but Bob had not been their first choice. Their first choice had taken another position, and Bob was the second choice of the committee and the third choice of the teachers. E-mails and phone calls had spread the word…the new principal was an unknown quantity. In addition, Bob was following a very unpopular principal who had not involved the faculty in any decision making. Curriculum decisions, scheduling, and student discipline policies had all been mandated with no discussion.

The teachers had become either complacent or hostile, and those attitudes had trickled down to the students. Bob had always loved a challenge and had led his former school to successful reform in climate, curriculum, and parental involvement. His leadership style was invitational, and he believed in modeling the behaviors he wanted his teachers to emulate.

Bob's first act was to invite the two teachers from the selection committee to breakfast and ask whether they would like to join him at a summer institute on school reform at a nearby college. He asked whether they could help him find others who would also be interested in attending the institute. He had negotiated additional staff development funds when he had taken the job, and he knew that he needed to establish a common vision among his staff. He also invited the current president of the parent association in his school.

Ten curious and skeptical teachers and one parent attended the institute with their new leader, and they got to know him as a person and an educator during those days together. Through participation with other schools and through the information given, they learned what was possible for their students and their school. They brainstormed with Bob how to share their information and new ideas with the rest of the staff. He suggested that each teacher share his or her experience with at least one other teacher at the same grade level.

Bob's first goal—to develop a shared vision—was well under way by the time school started. He had read James M. Kouzes and Barry Z. Posner's *The Leadership Challenge* (2002) and learned the five actions that they found (in a survey of more than 75,000 people) to be key for successful leadership. He modeled continuous learning and gave a small group a chance to develop a shared vision. According to Kouzes and Posner, in the first year, school leaders must challenge the processes that are in place, enable others to act, and encourage a rebirth of passion about students and teaching.

Bob knew that there would be many who would dare him to lead them during his first year as principal, and he felt ready to take the challenge with a group of supporters behind him. What he did not know was the degree of resistance that he would face or how to meet the resistance and increase the support base for change.

# Degrees of Followership

- ◆ Each of the rings in the circle may be a positive or negative force depending on the goals of the organization and leadership.
- ◆ Each ring of the circle may be an individual or a group.
- ◆ The size of the ring is proportional to the number of people in that ring.
- ◆ As the distance from the leadership (center) increases, there is less collaboration with the leader.
- ◆ The degrees of reluctance are the same whether the leadership is a person or a concept.

The following diagram illustrates the degrees of reluctance that followers portray.

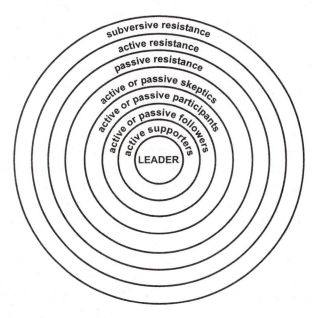

## Degrees of Reluctance Among Followers

- ◆ **Leader or concept:** The center of the circle represents the leader or the concept to be instituted. Though the principal is the acknowledged leader of the school, the school district may be attempting to implement the concept of block scheduling. Other concepts could be content areas, curriculum improvements, discipline, scheduling, or parental involvement. The leadership for the concept may be a person within the school, a team, or an outside consultant.

- **Active supporters:** The second ring comprises those who actively support the leader or the concept. They verbalize and actively participate in the progress of the person or the concept. They comfortably question the leadership and share a universal view of the purpose of the organization.

- **Active and passive followers:** The third ring is made up of active and passive followers who do their duty or job, support the leader or concept, and see their role as positive within the organization. They tend to let the leader do the thinking for them.

- **Active and passive participants:** The fourth ring consists of active and passive participants who simply do their job and do not interact with the leadership.

- **Active and passive skeptics:** The fifth level comprises both active and passive skeptics who do their job but question the leader and the concept. They tend to be supportive, but they may seriously question a single aspect of the leadership. They fluctuate between support and nonsupport depending on the issue. They use accurate data as their standard for support. Their skepticism may come from a lack of knowledge or skills.

- **Passive resistance:** In the sixth ring are those who practice passive resistance. They may require constant direction and reminders about the goals. They need constant supervision, as they frequently use old models and methods. They are more likely to do nothing than to support the leadership. However, they can be a powerful positive force in an organization that has a negative set of values. They may be quiet leaders, such as Gandhi, who value different methods of obtaining change.

- **Active resistance:** In the seventh ring are individuals or groups who actively resist change. They verbally attack the leadership and any new idea that comes along. They refuse to change what they are doing and try to get others to join them in resisting the leadership. They may plot against the leadership in the interest of what they perceive to be the good of the organization.

- **Subversive resistance:** The outermost circle includes those who quietly plan to get close to the leader, learn something that can be used against him or her or the concept, and then find others (like themselves) who will plot to overthrow the leadership. In schools, they listen to the mandates, say nothing to the leadership, and then close their classroom doors and do whatever they want. Subversive resistance may be necessary for a culture to survive a dictator or hostile leadership.

One goal of leadership is to break down the barriers that exist among the circles and to help all members of the organization move toward a positive goal. The key to the circle is that resistance is a matter of degree. It is a by-product of a communication system that is either functioning well or not. Creating an environment in which all followers can use their talents to meet the goals of the organization should be another goal of any leader. Leaders and followers are interrelated and should be able to move comfortably between the two roles. Most school leaders call this "getting everyone on board for the good of the kids."

Historically, school personnel thought that leaders should do all of the planning and that teachers should carry out their commands. There was both a real and assumed hierarchy of command, with the superintendent at the top and the students at the bottom. Those misperceptions became self-fulfilling prophecies, and teachers had little input into school goals until the concept of shared leadership emerged and was found to create better schools.

Process leadership assumes that a person or a group of people is in charge of an organization or a movement forward. Within the organization, there should be a group of supporters who form the inner circle of support and can be counted on to agree with the ideals and the ideas of the leadership. They may support the leadership for reasons related to trust, personal gain, or knowledge. They are more apt to be told essential information by the leadership. They are frequently called upon to lead aspects of the change.

## Success Story: One Who Took the Dare

This school leader has always built a strong, inclusive support base for his leadership. As a principal, superintendent, and university administrator, he has been a model for new administrators and a sought-after leadership consultant. Did he ever have reluctant followers? Of course he did.

He defines reluctant participants as ones who

- Fail to deliver effective instruction
- Intimidate students and fellow staff members
- Have "contract" paranoia—they are constantly wondering whether something they are being asked to consider is in the contract or not
- Are the first ones out the door after school
- Fail to care about students, themselves, or continuous improvement

- Are dishonest
- Breed pockets of resistance
- Are unwilling to do better work
- Display observable behaviors that are intimidating to their colleagues

This leader's strategies for working with these reluctant participants include the following:

- Establishing functional groups to be proactive with new ideas
- Working with the unsung heroes who show leadership
- Using good teachers as a method of passing information
- Using representative councils for decision making
- Using the council representatives as conduits in the building
- Calling in people and speaking with them one on one
- Letting people know that he is human
- Being honest when he makes a mistake
- Repairing mistakes immediately
- Listening to people who have opposing views—that is, biting his lip
- Working collectively to raise the bar for all students in the district, not just in his building
- Realizing that timing is everything and attending to issues raised by reluctant teachers immediately

This leader is known among his colleagues as a masterful public relations expert and a student advocate. He gets things done faster than most administrators with little reluctance. For example, he wanted to be sure that every student in his building had his or her picture on the assignment notebook that students are given each year. He assigned every homeroom a letter from the school name, Kimpton. When the day came for the picture to be taken, the students lined up in their letter formations on the playing field. Because he always included the community in the school's activities, a local pilot volunteered to fly over the field while another volunteer photographer took a picture of the group. Within days, the photo was developed, and every student appeared on the front of the assignment book. The teachers were amazed that such a big project could be done so easily, and it set the tone for many more.

Each homeroom was assigned a service group in the community. They were asked to make paper placemats listing positive things about their group. The students spent one homeroom period decorating the placemats, which were taken then to local Rotary, Lions, Masons, and church group meetings. Good news about the school was everywhere in the community.

As a principal, he made one decree: Every word that goes out of the building about our students must be stated in positive terms. That was his goal, and he asked his council of teachers how they could best implement that goal. He had tremendous support from parents because he required all teams of teachers to make two positive phone calls home each semester about each student, and he gave them time to do it. He modeled the same behavior by making phone calls himself and writing personal notes to all students.

Visitors to the school could feel its positive climate and see few reluctant staff members. This leader has been able to accomplish these things because he built a strong support base for his leadership.

When asked how he has built support, both as a principal and a superintendent, he said,

> I consistently had proactive groups that I worked with. As a superintendent, I had a group called Class Act that included all the bus drivers, custodians, cafeteria workers, and others whose jobs were listed as classified. I never called them noncertified as that is a negative term and I wanted to keep all communication positive. We met regularly to discuss issues and potential changes that were occurring. I found their input very important.

> I had another ongoing group called Pro-SAC. It was the made up of professionals from each building and was called the Superintendent's Advisory Council. I created opportunities for people to get together and talk about issues before we made any changes. I created groups as needs arose. I also had a curriculum council and a group called Presidents and Concerned Persons Council. This included presidents of local community groups such as the Rotary, the Lions, the PTA, and the teachers' union. Each building had two representatives and they had to be voted on by their colleagues to be there. Issues were brought up in a nonconfrontational climate. We gathered information together and there was awareness at every step of the way. We got the truth out before decisions were made and we headed off a lot of problems by just getting together.

> As the leader, I did a lot more listening than talking in all of these groups. Too often, leaders sit down with their inner circle, make a decision, and then ask for input. Others see through that and resent it. We need to legitimately make people part of what is going on. We have to remember that everyone has been to school and assume that everyone has good ideas when they make sug-

gestions. Sometimes people just ask us to consider the possibilities.

When someone is reluctant to change, you need to let them know that you know that they are not following the plan. Call them in, talk to them, and listen to them. Be upfront about your concerns. Make the improvement of instruction for kids the common denominator.

In his current position, this leader helps train new administrators. When asked what advice he gives them, he stated, "It is all about how you interact with the people you deal with."

- ◆ Leading is about relationships, relationships, and relationships.
- ◆ Lead by example. Be a lifelong learner. "I did a PowerPoint presentation for the first meeting with the faculty when I became the superintendent. PowerPoint wasn't really out yet, but I wanted them to be on the cutting edge of technology, so I had to demonstrate that I was," this leader said.
- ◆ Always strive to be better. An old coach once told this leader that he had a choice to get a little better or a little worse every day. When faculty members assumed that change meant they were bad or needed changing, he would tell them, "You don't have to be sick to get better."
- ◆ Use written evaluations to assess and change your leadership style. This leader's were done anonymously by the staff. In his school, all teachers were required to have students evaluate them anonymously once a year. The counselor would administer the forms. Teachers and administrators used the data for goal setting and improvement.
- ◆ Send handwritten letters of praise often—to students, staff, and parents.
- ◆ Be accessible. Having councils and advisory groups means that you must be accessible. Be available to students and staff during lunch.
- ◆ Let people know that you care about them.
- ◆ Read the work of Michael Fullan (2001) on changing school culture.

(Interview with Dr. John Haschak, 2006.)[1]

This success story is just one of many gathered for this book. The leaders interviewed for this book are all leaders who have made observable differences in the schools in which they work. They all have unique and successful ways of dealing with reluctant followers. Their stories and examples were given humbly, with nothing more than a desire to be helpful to others.

The chapters that follow define the characteristics of reluctant followers, their personality types, leadership styles, communication strategies, and motivations. Successful school leaders were observed and interviewed over the past two decades as they implemented change within their schools and among their followers. The stories of ordinary leaders making extraordinary changes are told in each chapter. They are leaders who have quietly led their schools through changes that positively affected the lives and learning of their students. Their valuable insights and actions define a pattern of school leadership that can be emulated by all.

## Resources

Bjugstad, K., Thach, E. C., Thompson, K. J., & Morris, A. (2006). A fresh look at followership: A model for matching followership and leadership styles. *Journal of Behavioral and Applied Management, 7*(3), 304–319.

Collins, J. C. (2001). *Good to great: Why some companies make the leap—and others don't.* New York: HarperBusiness.

Fleck, F. (2005). *What successful principals do: 169 tips for principals.* Larchmont, NY: Eye On Education.

Fullan, M. (1993). *Change forces: Probing the depths of educational reform.* London: Falmer Press.

Fullan, M. (2001). *Leading in a culture of change.* San Francisco: Jossey-Bass.

Haschak, J. (2006, June). Interview with the author, Ashland, OH.

Kelley, R. E. (1988). In praise of followers. *Harvard Business Review, 66*(6), 142–148.

Kelley, R. E. (1992). *The power of followership: How to create leaders people want to follow, and followers who lead themselves.* New York: Doubleday/Currency.

Kouzes, J. M., & Posner, B. Z. (2002). *The leadership challenge* (3rd ed.). San Francisco: Jossey-Bass.

Moller, G., & Pankake, A. (2006). *Lead with me: A principal's guide to teacher leadership.* Larchmont, NY: Eye On Education.

Whitaker, T. (2003). *What great principals do differently.* Larchmont, NY: Eye On Education.

[1]Dr. John Haschak is currently the Resident Director of Graduate Studies at Ashland University in Massellon, Ohio.

# 2

# Identifying Reluctant Followers: Who Are They and Why Do They Refuse to Follow the Leader?

Ensuring academic success for every student was a necessary and improbable goal for the new principal of a middle school that had reading scores two years below the state norm for 40% of the students. Attendance (both students and staff) and test scores were low. As the principal met the faculty for the first time as a group, the unsmiling faces, folded arms, and stoic postures gave the impression that this was a group that would often say, "Lead me—I dare you."

Every leader of an organization finds there are certain personalities within a group who refuse to follow. Reluctant followers hamper the effectiveness of the leader and keep the organization from moving forward or solving problems. Few leaders are employed to maintain the status quo, but there are many comfortable people within organizations who believe that it is their job to maintain business as usual.

Educational leaders usually assume a set of universal values that are shared by the staff, students, and parents. They want to see their staff have a shared vision and work toward it for the sake of their students. A culture of communication, caring, concern, and commitment is usually written into every school mission statement. However, all of these assumptions and plans may hit a brick wall during the first staff meeting when changes are proposed.

Federal mandates such as the No Child Left Behind Act, state achievement testing, university accreditation, local school board directives, building needs assessments, and special interest groups can all require that an educational leader effect change within his or her organization. Whether the leader is a university president, a dean, a department chair, a superintendent, a principal, or a team leader, he or she is charged with following the law and designing, organizing, and implementing an environment in which students can learn. All leaders want to develop a positive culture in which learning can take place. They may or may not be the chosen leader of the group.

## Why Leaders Are Not Followed

People who do not follow the leader may have a vision of the future that does not match that of the leadership or management. They may have had experiences with past leaders that have caused them to develop an attitude of mistrust. They may feel that leadership should be shared among all involved in an organization or task. Others are just stuck in a rut, and they are hostile toward any change that is mentioned. Some have language difficulties, nonwork issues, or past grievances with the organization. No matter what the reason, their refusal to participate takes a great deal of time for the person in the leadership position and affects the culture of the organization.

Some show their unwillingness to cooperate verbally, whereas others stand back and give the leader the look that says, "Lead me—I dare you." They are skeptics who may eventually follow the leader to the goal. While leaders in government, business, and industry expect that adults will follow them, they go to great lengths to ensure success and profit. They can offer bonus packages, incentives, and promotions.

Reluctant followers can be transferred or fired. The best-seller list always includes the newest thinking in management. The most significant difference between those organizations and schools is that corporations do not have the long-term impact on the future of children that schools have. School leadership affects the daily lives of families and communities. School success means a stronger society in the future.

School leadership has many levels that can face reluctant followers. The superintendent, school board, principals, classroom teachers, team leaders, and student leadership all make decisions that affect the culture of the school district and the students who learn there. At each of those levels, there are reluctant followers.

As a result of observation and participation at faculty meetings, in-service workshops, strategic planning sessions, and school board meetings, we have concluded that there are consistent reasons for reluctant following in the school setting.

## 10 Reasons Why School Personnel Don't Follow the Leader

Reluctant followers refuse to participate, change, or cooperate for 10 basic reasons:

1. They dislike or mistrust the leader.
2. They have a different belief system than the leader.
3. They have a limited or different vision of the future.
4. They believe in the old adage "If it ain't broke, don't fix it."
5. They are loyal to a former leader who implemented the current program.
6. They have personal issues that are affecting their ability to participate.
7. They are planning to leave the organization within a short period of time.
8. They have not received adequate communication.
9. They are, by nature, uncooperative with others.
10. They do not have the skills to do what the leader is proposing.

Some followers encompass all of these reasons, whereas others may have only one or two. The degree to which followers disagree with the leader depends on many variables in their own personality and experience. Whether the person to be followed is in business, a community volunteer position, a religious organization, a team, or a school, the reasons are the same.

The school, as a community, faces the same challenges to leadership that any other business faces. Schools are constantly asked by their clients—the public and the students—to change. Societal needs dictate challenges to the curriculum, organization, and personnel every day.

# Characteristics of Resistant Followers

If school leaders propose large-scale school reforms or changes to schedules, curricula, organizational patterns, or commonly held rituals, they may encounter the following personalities (Bergmann & Maute, 1999):

- **Ben There and his buddy, Don That:** These two band together to make sure the status quo is maintained. As soon as any change is put up for consideration and study, they stand and deliver a speech that is already familiar to other faculty members. They cite the one time they tried something new and it did not work. They are famous for recalling all of the negative aspects of any changes that actually did take place. Their comfort level as teachers is threatened by new leadership and any change. They assume that they are leaders among the faculty, but they have few followers.

- **Willie Fold:** Willie has been on the faculty longer than anyone else, and he has been using the same curriculum, tests, and assignments for 30 years. He figures that he can outlast any new idea—that most leaders will give up after trying to get him to change. He thinks of new leadership as a card game in which he holds all the trump cards. After all, he has outlasted six principals.

- **Ima Rumor:** Whatever is spoken by the leader or followers is spread rapidly by this faculty member. The truth is not as important as the assumption, and all rumors are spread as if they were true. This person causes much lost time for the leader, as fires are constantly being fanned and need to be put out.

- **Ben A. Leader:** This person was in a leadership position in the building in the past and holds several grudges because he was not followed. Ben makes sure that if he is not followed, no one will be followed. He sabotages every idea by forming alliances with his few remaining friends in the building. He spends more time trying to form alliances than he does teaching.

- **Ina Hurry:** This follower thrives on change and loves change for change's sake. Unfortunately, she likes any change, regardless of whether it is good for the system. She jumps on every bandwagon that comes along and pushes others so hard that they resist the leader instead of her.

- **Samantha (Sam) Sarcasm:** She is the most negative of the followers. She is sarcastic to her colleagues, leaders, and students. Every idea that is expressed is fodder for her sarcastic remarks and jokes. She monopolizes meetings by causing stress among participants.

She uses her sarcasm to avoid being chosen for committees and having to change.

- **Noah Substance:** Noah works in the organization, but he has no idea what is going on and does not care. He does only what he has to do—no more. He has never proposed a new idea, supported an idea, or participated in any change. He couldn't care less who the leader is, as he follows no one—except the voices in his head.

- **Tota Lee Complacent:** Tota Lee couldn't care less what happens in the school. She has no opinion on any issue and wants to be left alone in her classroom, where she does as little teaching as possible. She, too, avoids faculty discussions, never volunteers, and does the minimum necessary to keep her job. New leadership does not bother her because she simply does not care. (Bergmann & Maute, 1999)

Many others are skeptical followers, and skepticism is not necessarily a negative thing for leadership. Too many leaders who are authoritarian, laissez-faire, or incapable have created these skeptical followers. Adults who follow are not like the children in the game Follow the Leader. Sometimes a leader marches in with a great idea and everyone cheers, other times they look back and no one is following. Ideally, every leader would lead a group that is made up of Ima Learners:

- **Ima Learner:** Ima is a joy to lead, as she is willing to research, work, and communicate with others in the group. She volunteers to be on steering committees and thrives on change. She asks thoughtful questions and encourages discussion of issues. She mentors newcomers and challenges skeptics. She follows when necessary and leads when called upon to do so.

But many Imas in a school keep quiet because they are intimidated by the other reluctant followers. Too often, the Imas silently support the leader as they listen and learn. So what happens when a new leader faces all of the reluctant followers just described?

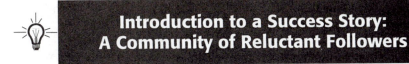

## Introduction to a Success Story: A Community of Reluctant Followers

She was transferred within the district because of her success as a leader and change agent in her former middle school. Her reward, as is often the case, was to be given an even tougher school to turn around. This school, with its low test scores, poor student attendance, minimal parent participation, and staff that had survived three former principals in five years, would need a courageous, collaborative leader to make a difference. She needed to take definitive action that would show all of the constituents that she meant to affect change in this school. She met with students, parents, and staff members, who gave input on the needs of the school. She reviewed the records of students and staff members to get an accurate picture of where she should start.

She started by meeting with the principals of the six feeder schools to establish a picture of the students who would be entering her school for the first time. By the time the staff met for the first official day of school, she had determined that she would need to collaborate with the staff, set a common vision, and make that happen immediately.

The staff was used to waiting out each new principal who had a new idea. They had been successful for the past five years, and they did not know why this time should be any different. She was not prepared for the complacent and hostile staff that stared back at her during the first meeting. Though they smiled and nodded politely when she spoke, their body language said, "Lead me—I dare you."

Before school started, she met individuals on an informal basis who were professional and willing to share information about the procedures of the school; however, she was not prepared for the collective dare given by the group. Within one faculty, she had inherited the following:

- The former principal, who had been given a job as a social studies teacher
- Seven teachers who had been in the building for at least 10 years
- Four new first-year teachers
- Dysfunctional teams with common planning periods
- A new block schedule
- Exploratory teachers who saw the students for nine weeks
- Three teachers who had been denied transfers within the district
- A secretary who believed that she ran the building
- A part-time school nurse
- Two counselors with student loads of 450 each
- As assistant principal who did not get the job as principal, even though he was the faculty favorite

Leaders who inherit such cultures usually analyze the school culture and assess the degree of resistance and degree of acceptance. This analysis should be done by talking to the people who work in the building. Much can be learned by talking to the clients of the organization as well.

When students in this dysfunctional school were interviewed, they noted that the school would be a lot better if the faculty members would stop fighting with each other. They articulated why some teachers did not teach and why many did not care. They felt that the school was not a good place to be. Any effort at student input had been met with resistance from former leaders.

Several leaders had tried to change the culture, but the staff harbored such strong feelings against each other that it affected the students' behavior in a negative way. The new leadership eventually had to ask for many personnel transfers within the district. Those extreme measures were the only thing that allowed reform to begin to take place in the building. More on this story later.

Other followers expect the leader to maintain the status quo and refrain from rocking the boat. If changes are anticipated, reluctant followers dig in their heels and try to gather forces against the anticipated change.

Most reluctant followers have a perception of their own worth in the school, which may be threatened by the unknown qualities that the new leader beings. A principal who expects teams to meet and use their planning time effectively may be surprised by their current practices. Talented teachers who have not been recognized may not use their skills for fear of reprisal from colleagues.

In addition to the different types of reluctant followers, their degrees of reluctance, their expectations of leadership, and their history in the organization, leaders must consider how and when reluctant followers make their dare.

## When Do Reluctant Followers Display Their Reluctance?

◆ **In private conversations:** Some reluctant followers speak privately with the leader about their reluctance and attempt to find common ground. Others thrive on stating their opposition to the leadership in a public forum. The timing usually depends on whether the reluctance is the result of personality or purpose. If the reluctance is caused by personality differences, the timing will depend on what the follower hopes to gain.

◆ **During large group decision-making gatherings (without the prior knowledge of the leader):** A follower who hopes to gain personal notoriety will speak out in meetings for the purpose of getting his or her own ideas across before the leader has any idea that he or she is proposing something new or contrary. These blindsiding speeches by wannabe leaders are often challenged by the group because they are poorly timed and have no group purpose. For example, one college professor never asked a question or raised an issue during months of discussion about new standards. On the day of the final faculty vote, he spent 20 minutes sharing an alternate proposal. Although the leader listened to his proposal, the professor was chastised by his peers for his poor attempt at subversive resistance. This type of leadership filibuster usually strengthens the leader within the group. Adults can sense when a person is posturing for leadership and does not have the goals of the organization in mind.

♦ **In small group sessions:** A follower who hopes to offer alternative proposals for change or leadership may also target small groups in an attempt to gather his or her own support group. The follower looks for teachers who are vulnerable or insecure in their jobs. For example, one high school teacher was so opposed to block scheduling that she presented a list of 10 reasons why it would not work to every department in the school, but she used 16 personal planning periods to do so. Although she gathered a few followers, the rest of the faculty, who had been working on research committees for the idea, saw her tactics as divisive and ineffective.

♦ **On the fly...in the hall, in the parking lot, in the lunchroom, at the copy machine, at the barbershop, at a local service group gathering, or at a basketball game:** This type of reluctant follower likes to gossip and fuel the fires of dissent by coercing coworkers, parents, or community members one on one. He or she uses personal examples and targets those who are new to the organization. For example, one new teacher was actually threatened by two veteran teachers to "not get too chummy with the administration," and another was told to stop being so creative because she was making the rest of the teachers look bad. Others who dissent on the fly may have a particular political bone to pick with the organization, and they may seek out other dissidents in this way. Their political purpose is much different from those who do not follow because they have a personal issue with the leadership.

Leaders must be sensitive to and aware of the timing of reluctant followers and confront their concerns privately before the reluctance escalates and spreads. At the same time, leaders must develop a support base among those who are in favor of the proposed changes, such as Ima Learner.

## Common Myths Among Reluctant Followers

Several myths are common among reluctant followers. They make the dare to leadership because they believe

◆ The leader is using his or her position as a stepping stone to a higher position

◆ The leader has an inner circle of people who make all of the decisions

◆ There is really no a crisis or reason to change

◆ There is no accountability for their actions

◆ No one really cares what they think or do

◆ Difficult tasks are threats rather than challenges

◆ Leaders can perform miracles all by themselves

## Strong Followers, Weak Leaders

Some highly motivated followers will dare the leadership just to get them motivated. For example, one middle school had a group of teachers who wanted to form teams, but the principal was afraid that the majority would balk at the idea and create conflict. He did not like conflict in any way and spent most of his time trying to avoid it. When the group asked to go to visit a school that used teams, he reluctantly allowed them to go but did not go along. When they asked to report on their findings at a faculty meeting, he reluctantly agreed and gave them a few minutes at the end of the meeting.

When they asked to pilot a team during the second semester, he said it was impossible to schedule. When they showed him how it could be done without affecting anyone else, he agreed. Their enthusiasm and success with students was contagious, and soon another group of teachers were asking to team. Although a few reluctant teachers did not want to team, the majority asked whether they could arrange the schedule for teaming and get some training. As he gave in—to avoid conflict—he realized that he had better find out more about the concept. The teacher leadership in his building was stronger than his own leadership, and it motivated him to learn about the change process.

Followers can make as big a difference as leaders when they are given time, choices, and opportunities. There are hundreds of examples of schools in which strong faculty leaders have maintained good programs for students and effected positive change while a parade of weak, ineffective leaders marches through the main office. Other strong leaders have recognized the potential of developing teachers as leaders and given them many varied opportunities. According to Gayle Moller and Anita Pankake, "Principals who build relationships with informal teacher leaders can set in motion incredible accomplishments, such as establishing procedures for safe school, designing a tutorial program, or building parent-community programs. There is not limit to the opportunities for informal teacher leaders to take action" (2006, p. 163).

So how do all of these reluctant followers who dare the leadership interact within a school setting? What can be gained by encouraging teachers to participate in the planning process? Let's go back to our middle school principal with the enormous challenge.

## Success Story: Developing a Common Vision and Mission in a Community of Followers

The principal with the overwhelming task of turning around a large middle school and raising reading scores wanted to develop a vision of what the school could become. She was aware of the degree of reluctance she faced because she had had one-on-one conversations with every faculty member. She had asked them to help her understand their vision of the purpose and goals of the school.

During her initial attempts to determine the faculty's vision for the school, she found that so many teachers were trying to survive day to day that they had very little vision except more help and more money. She had her own vision of what was possible, but it was a vision of process rather than product. She found that the reluctant followers were very product oriented. They wanted to solve a specific problem and then return to the status quo. For example, they wanted to raise test scores in reading, but they did not want to deal with the systemic problems affecting the students. Their expectation was simply to spend more time on reading, regardless of whether the practices were effective. They were doing something regardless of whether it was working or not.

# Developing a Shared Vision

The first step toward developing a shared vision is to invite all stakeholders to be a part of the visioning process. Our principal invited not only staff but also parents, students, and community members to join her in establishing a three-year plan of action. She made sure that all of the groups in the building were represented on a Vision Task Force. Then, she implemented the following process:

- ◆ She stated the purpose of the visioning process: to improve collaboration and communication among members of the school community.

- ◆ She asked each staff member and committee member to write a belief statement answering the following questions: What do I believe about young adolescents? What do I believe about educating young adolescents?

- ◆ She offered copies of *This We Believe in Action: Implementing Successful Middle Level Schools* (2005), published by the National Middle School Association, as an example of how belief statements should be written and to share the generally accepted beliefs about educating this age group.

- ◆ She established focus groups to gather input from staff members, parents, students, and the community about what they wanted the school to become. The focus groups discussed the following questions:

  - • What is the status of our school right now? How do we know that status?

  - • How does the current status of our school affect our students?

  - • What do we believe is possible for our students?

  - • What would we like to keep in our school? What would we like to drop from our school? What would we like to change about our school?

  - • What research supports what we are doing?

  - • What do we need to do immediately for our students? What should be our long-term goal?

  - • What are other schools doing to maintain and develop curriculum standards, climate, etc.?

  - • What do we need to do in order to move toward a collective vision?

- She collected the focus group data and shared those data with the committee and staff.

- She identified the school's top five needs from the focus group data.

- She gave two reluctant followers the task of completing shadow studies of two students. They were to choose a student at random and follow that student for an entire school day, logging what the student was doing every five minutes. The goal was to give the teachers an idea of what life was like for students in the school. They were to share their findings with the entire staff.

- She shared accurate demographic data with the staff and committee and had them develop a list of the top 10 student needs based on the data. That data were compiled and communicated to the students. The students were asked to give their input on the list and make any changes.

- The committee drafted a vision statement that was distributed to the staff, students, and parents for input.

- After several drafts, a vision statement was accepted by all of the groups and approved by the board of education.

- The vision statement was printed and posted throughout the building as a constant reminder of the school's vision.

As she saw some of the staff's reluctance waning—because they were actually giving input—she also noticed that the skepticism of others was increasing. Conversations with these people indicated that they were afraid that all of this work was all talk and that no action would actually be taken.

She explained that the second phase of the visioning process was action planning and that it would begin the same week.

## Action Planning

- Each need that was identified by the focus group and shadow study data became the topic of study for an action committee.

- Action committee goals were written by the original Vision Task Force.

- Teachers, students, parents, and community members were invited to volunteer for these committees. Groups of 8–10 people were chosen for each committee. Reluctant followers were personally invited to participate in a group.

- Each committee was given the task of researching solutions to the problem. They were given access to research, literature, and consultants. They were allowed to visit other schools that had solved the same problem. For example, because reading was such an issue, one committee looked at the reading programs of similar schools, wrote to schools that had been successful, and asked a large group of current students for suggestions.

As the reluctant followers saw the data-gathering process at work and actively participated in it, they were assured that the results would benefit their students.

- When the research was completed, each group wrote a proposal of how to change or implement some aspect of their topic in the school. Some problems required minimal administrative changes, whereas others required staff development and changes in attitudes and practices.

- A budget was attached to each proposal, and possibilities for grants were noted whenever applicable.

- All proposals were presented to the Vision Task Force and then ranked in order of student need.

- A final ranking and proposed timeline that included all of the proposals was created. A tentative budget was attached.

- The proposal was presented to the entire staff for input. They were given one week to reply and make suggestions.

- The suggestions were read and tabulated. The Vision Task Force added those that were realistic to the proposals.

- A final proposal was written by the Vision Task Force and presented to the board of education for action.

- The proposal was refined to include the board's suggestions, and a three-year timeline was established for the implementation of proposals.

- Changes to the reading curriculum became the immediate goal.

- The final proposal was taken to the school board for action and support.

- Skeptics and reluctant followers were present at the board meeting to help present the visioning proposal.

Although a few remained reluctant for personal reasons that had nothing to do with school, most of those who had been reluctant followers had become immersed in the planning process and felt a sense of ownership in its success.

As this process evolved, the principal heard more and more conversations about student needs and saw more and more interaction among the staff. The immediate decision to offer more reading time and materials to students gave credibility to the work of the committees and the entire process.

When the skeptics saw action taking place, they began to move toward active participation rather than passive or active resistance. Because they were constantly being invited to participate in the process, their reluctance dwindled, and more teachers became involved. To those who were still resistant, the principal explained,

- There was a process in place for school improvement.
- The process required the involvement of the entire staff for the good of the students.
- If they truly felt that they had a value conflict with the process and the proposals, that they should seek transfers within the district.

Her willingness to confront the resistance had a huge impact on trust within the building. More and more teachers became active supporters of the process. The principal never made the process reliant on her personal leadership. Teachers were chosen as leaders for the implementation of the proposals. Within two years, reading scores were making steady positive gains at all grade levels, the truancy rate had dropped from 16% to 3%, teachers were beginning to use teaming to help students, and the climate of the building had become civil and productive.

(Interview with a middle school principal.)

## Success Story: From a Teacher's Point of View

In a different school that also went through a visioning process, a teacher who was a part of the planning committee became a learning coordinator in the building. She was charged with the actual implementation of the curriculum changes, scheduling changes, pilot programs, and staff development. She faced reluctance on a daily basis as teachers tried new methods and faced longer class periods because of the block schedule.

She was so successful in helping to make systemic change in her building that when she retired, she became a change consultant for several large educational organizations.

Reflecting on her career as a teacher, team leader, learning coordinator, and now consultant, she noted that in leading people to change, a leader must

- Be clear about the purpose of the change
- Be clear about what they should expect and how the process will unfold

◆ Be patient

As she has watched leaders make significant change, she has observed several practices of good leaders:

- ◆ Leaders focus the proposed change on a clearly defined purpose and refer back to that purpose frequently.
- ◆ Leaders thread best practices research throughout the work by forming study groups and sharing personal examples.
- ◆ Leaders target supporters and solicit their support. They let peer pressure work on reluctant participants.
- ◆ Leaders establish leadership teams and involve everyone in the decision making. Input is sought frequently.
- ◆ Leaders frequently evaluate what has been done and celebrate any progress that has been made.
- ◆ Leaders catch reluctant staff members being good and build on their strengths. This uncovering of greatness seemed to be a key to significant personal change on the part of many reluctant followers.

As this teacher began working with many different schools she noticed that those who were most reluctant did not have a "students first" or "learning never ends" mind-set. They were experienced teachers who believed that what they were doing was working—and in many cases, it was. They did not feel a need to try a new strategy just because it might help a few more students. They were not thoroughly grounded in best practices or the developmental characteristics of adolescents. They were content-area specialists with little knowledge of what makes teenagers learn. They did not make "what's best for kids" the focal point of their decision making. Most were on overload, thinking that "this too shall pass." They saw any change as a phase or a pet project of the new administration and felt that it would soon pass, so why get involved?

This team leader was successful not only with her team and her school but also has helped countless others make classroom changes by making connections and building relationships with them. She persists in her optimism, but she does not bulldoze the ideas of others. They know that she has a teacher's perspective—she understands what it is like to have 150 students a day and papers to grade while trying to implement something new.

She gives them options or choices whenever possible and seeks them out for advice on particular issues.

Her advice to leaders is sound and well respected:

- Every culture has reluctant followers. Some are products of the culture, and some create their own reluctance by getting into a rut. They may or may not know how to get out.
- Leaders must tell people why change is necessary, solicit input and form study groups, listen to their concerns, offer examples of success whenever possible, and be clear about what is expected.
- Timelines, patience, and constant reminders that the change is for the students are all essential elements in helping reluctant followers.

(Interview with Linda Holdorf, 2006.)[1]

## Summary

Change in a school or in the leadership of a school can create reluctant followers. There are many types of personalities that exhibit this reluctance. Recognizing of the types of reluctant followers, the degree of their reluctance, and the timing of their expressions of reluctance can help leaders decide how to lead. When reluctance meets shared leadership and a visioning process, it can be decreased. School leaders who implement vision committees and follow an action planning process can limit the number of reluctant participants in their school.

## Resources

Bergmann, S., & Maute, J. (1999). *Who killed staff development?* Presentation to the National Middle School Association.

Erb, T. O. (Ed.). (2005). *This we believe in action: Implementing successful middle level schools.* Westerville, OH: National Middle School Association.

Holdorf, L. (2006). Interview with the author.

Lounsbury, J. (Ed.). (1999). *This we believe.* Westerville, OH: National Middle School Association.

Moller, G., & Pankake, A. (2006). *Lead with me: A principal's guide to teacher leadership.* Larchmont, NY: Eye On Education.

Whitaker, T., Whitaker, B., & Lumpa, D. (2000). *Motivating and inspiring teachers: The educational leader's guide for building staff morale.* Larchmont, NY: Eye On Education.

[1]Linda Holdorf is currently Educational Consultant for the Turning Points Project with the Association of Illinois Middle Schools and lives in Naperville, IL.

# 3

# Assessing the Impact
# of Personality on Leading
# and Following

The principal left the faculty meeting quietly shaking her head. The same teacher as usual had sat through the meeting doing the daily crossword puzzle. Another one, who apparently had not prepared for the meeting, had come in late, and her state of fluster had distracted the rest of the faculty members. How would she deal with these uncooperative teachers? How would she find a way to involve them and use their talents and skills?

If I do not want what you want, please try not to tell me that my want is wrong.

Or if I believe other than you, at least pause before you correct my view.

Or if my emotion is less than yours, or more, given the same circumstances, try not to ask me to feel more strongly or weakly.

Or yet if I act, or fail to act, in the manner of your design for action, let me be.

I do not, for the moment at least, ask you to understand me. That will come only when you are willing to give up changing me into a copy of you.

—David Keirsey, *Please Understand Me II*

In Chapter 2, we met some of the personality types that we must deal with on a regular basis. This chapter presents additional information on personality types and tests and how they can be used to identify the talents and strengths of reluctant followers.

## Personality Types

We all know that different personality types exist. Some of us are very directive but not good listeners. Some of us value time constraints, whereas others feel limited by them. And some of us follow the rules, whereas others don't even read the rules. How on earth can we form an effective school community if we can't even understand each other?

It would be helpful for the school staff (including the principal) to take the Keirsey Temperament Sorter (http://www.keirsey.com) or a version of the Myers-Briggs Type Indicator (http://www.humanmetrics.com/cgi-win/JTypes2.asp). Whereas the latter describes 16 different combinations of personality types, Keirsey identifies just four distinctive personality types and explains some of the behaviors of each type. When one educational leader used the Temperament Sorter with her staff, teachers began to talk with one another about their differences. A guardian personality, who is directive, organized, logical, impatient, and always on time, began to understand an artisan personality, who is more laid back, creative, a bit disorganized, and constantly in motion. All of the types that Keirsey defines—guardians, artisans, rationals, and idealists—bring to the table different talents and difficulties. But it is not until we understand each other that we can begin to be able to work together constructively.

Astute leaders will place idealists, who like harmony and work well in cooperative situations, with rationals, who need to see a specific reason for their work. Rationals need to be convinced that their work is meaningful and visionary. Both the Keirsey and Human Metrics Web sites allow participants to take a short online test and receive a printed description of their particular personality type. Teachers find it fascinating. The discussion that occurs when faculty members explain how they operate to others illuminates the differences between some teachers' expectations not only of their colleagues but of their students as well. It is only when we come to understand the nature of others and ourselves that we can begin to work with them harmoniously.

Such discussions also foster a sense of trust. We may all be different, but we're in this together. We must stop judging others and start to embrace our differences. Because students also have different personality types, we need different types of teachers to help us understand some students' behaviors and attitudes. The diversity of teachers' personality types needs to be viewed as beneficial for meeting the needs of a diverse student body.

In the same way, a savvy leader will help followers to understand the multiple intelligences described by Howard Gardner (1983). A Google search will reveal many different intelligence surveys. One can be found at http://www.ldrc.ca, a Web site that facilitates work with people with learning disabilities. One of the benefits of taking such an indicator is that it helps to build strong teams of teachers with different strengths to better meet the needs of diverse students. It will also help leaders assign appropriate tasks to their faculty so as to take advantage of their abilities.

## Emotional Intelligence

Daniel Goleman (1998) defines emotional intelligence as "the capacity for recognizing our own feelings and those of others, for motivating ourselves, and for managing emotions well in ourselves and in our relationships." Goleman describes the ways in which people comprehend and act on certain circumstances because of their emotional intelligence. He and the Hay Group, with whom he collaborates, claim that emotional intelligence can be improved, thus enhancing job performance. The components of emotional intelligence are as follows:

- ◆ Self-awareness: Knowing one's internal states, preferences, resources, and intuitions
  - Emotional awareness: Recognizing one's emotions and their effects
  - Accurate self-assessment: Knowing one's strengths and limits
  - Self-confidence: Having a strong sense of one's self-worth and capabilities
- ◆ Self-management: Managing ones' internal states, impulses, and resources
  - Emotional self-control: Keeping disruptive emotions and impulses in check
  - Transparency: Maintaining integrity and acting in congruence with one's values
  - Adaptability: Remaining flexible in handling change
  - Achievement orientation: Striving to improve or meet a standard of excellence
  - Initiative: Displaying a readiness to act on opportunities

- Optimism: Persisting in pursuing goals despite obstacles and setbacks

Social competencies, another part of emotional intelligence, determine how we handle relationships:

- ◆ Social awareness: Being aware of others' feelings, needs, and concerns
  - Empathy: Sensing others' feelings and perspectives and taking an active interest in their concerns
  - Organizational awareness: Reading a group's emotional currents and power relationships
  - Service orientation: Anticipating, recognizing, and meeting customers' needs
- ◆ Relationship management: Inducing desirable responses in others
  - Developing others: Sensing others' developmental needs and bolstering their abilities
  - Inspirational leadership: Inspiring and guiding individuals and groups
  - Influence: Wielding effective tactics for persuasion
  - Change catalyst: Initiating or managing change
  - Conflict management: Negotiating and resolving disagreements
  - Teamwork and collaboration: Working with others toward shared goals, creating group synergy in pursuing collective goals (retrieved August 2006, from http://ei.haygroup.com/about_ei/)

A short online quiz is available at http://www.ei.haygroup.com.

## Understanding the Personal Issues of Reluctant Followers

Many times, there is a personal issue affecting the personality of a follower that cannot be measured or assessed because it is life altering. Some of the issues that should be considered when assessing reluctance in followers include the following:

- ◆ Personal chronic illness
- ◆ Life-threatening illness of self or a family member
- ◆ Need to care for an elderly parent

- Divorce or marital difficulties
- Financial problems
- A combination of all of the above

The only way to determine whether such an issue is creating the reluctance is to invite people to talk to you about why they are not involving themselves in the process of change. Unless the follower is willing to confide in the leader, he or she may be seen as simply a resistant personality. Teachers who are frequently absent and miss meetings may be facing issues outside school that are much more important to them than what is going on in school. A leader who is approachable, compassionate, and caring will know about these personal issues. If a one-on-one conference is held between the leader and the reluctant follower, the leader can simply ask the staff member why he or she is not displaying his or her usual energy and enthusiasm for the proposed changes.

## Cultural, Racial, and Gender Differences

As the demographics of our society change, leaders must be able to help their community members cooperate with others who come from different cultures and backgrounds. Too often, communication problems are the result of misread signals. Leaders are encouraged to have open dialogue about cultural, racial, and gender differences, a difficult subject to address.

Juan Lopez-Campillo (n.d.) writes, "Why is an open dialogue helpful? Many people are uncomfortable talking about differences, and many people are unfamiliar with cultures or backgrounds that are different from their own. An open dialogue provides an opportunity for employees of different backgrounds to learn about each other, which, in turn, can decrease misunderstandings, enhance communication, and increase productivity."

Often, people who come to the United States from other countries have different conceptions of time and personal space. Whereas Americans tend to value time and consider lateness a real flaw, many Asian, Latin American, and African American cultures have a more fluid conception of time. Americans regard personal space as sacrosanct (recall your last elevator ride), whereas many other cultures feel that it is perfectly natural to get up close and personal. Many leaders in our society are fairly informal—teachers call them by their first names, and leaders often have open-door policies. However, other cultures may find such informality insulting and, as a result, view such leaders as weak. Even eye contact is viewed positively in some cultures but is considered disrespectful in others.

Such conflicts of values can prove to be disastrous in a collaborative working group, in a relationship between a leader and coworker, or in a teacher–student relationship. Open and honest dialogue among leaders and staff will help bring these different perspectives to light. Leaders may have to ask specific questions and listen carefully to the responses. According to Lopez-Campillo, open dialogue helps in the following ways:

- Enhances sensitivity to and fosters a better understanding of differences

- Provides a safe environment in which to explore the way that perceptions, stereotypes, and assumptions about people who are different from oneself limit effectiveness and communications

- Examines and dispels old myths

- Helps individuals move away from old behaviors that equate differences with "less than" or "inferior"

The American workplace has been dominated by male leaders for decades. Although the statistics are changing, most superintendents and school principals tend to be men. We have become used to a male leadership style. Gender differences can construct communication barriers. Men and women approach the workplace very differently. Men tend to be more directive, but when women are equally directive, they are perceived as "bossy." Women tend to ask more questions than men and tend to soften their directives with phrases such as "if you don't mind." Such behaviors, though too often viewed as signs of weakness, can be effective leadership strategies in a collaborative workplace. Again, open dialogue can help to overcome stereotypes and misunderstandings. We need to put these issues on the table and deal with them head on.

## Tips for Dealing With Difficult People

The Institute for Management Excellence (1999) offers the following tips for dealing with difficult people:

- When you see someone go into attack mode or display excess defensiveness, recognize that it is useless to argue with him or her. Wait until heads have cooled and listen to the involved parties to determine the basis for such a heated disagreement. Often, disputes are caused by miscommunication or misunderstanding. Listening is a crucial skill for effective leaders.

- Realize that the person is feeling very insecure. Animals of all types attack when they feel threatened. Change in schools is now a routine process. It seems impossible to keep following the same old routine, but some people rely on that routine to feel good about themselves. Effective leaders need to support teachers in other ways when a routine is removed.

♦ Don't continue to push a difficult person, as he or she will only get worse. Often, angry people forget the source of their anger and let it build for its own sake. Back off and give the person space. Tell him or her that you'll talk at a later time, when you've both had time to reflect on the issue.

♦ If the symptoms only seem to occur when the person is under stress, wait until another time to pursue the discussion. Work out gimmicks that everyone (including students) can use when their tolerance is low. For example, one teacher created a stoplight with red, amber, and green construction paper lights. When he put the red dot on the traffic light, the students knew to tread lightly.

♦ Keep your own sense of self-confidence and don't allow yourself to be verbally abused. Although it is easier to say than do, arguments can't be taken as personal assaults. Always try to stick to the issue rather than the individuals involved.

♦ Help the person see how much his or her negative behavior is damaging potential and working relationships. Negative–negative people often don't realize how they are perceived. Some realize it but don't seem to care. Heart-to-heart talks about enjoying our work and being good role models for students often help build more positive attitudes.

♦ Set goals for the person to learn to work better with others and monitor his or her behavior until it improves. Self-reflection and goal setting are essential to attitude adjustment. We all need to evaluate our behavior in light of different contexts: What choices did I make? Why did I make them? Could I have acted differently and brokered a different more positive result? What goals should I set for myself to become a more participatory and helpful part of my professional team? Leaders need to listen to teachers' self-reflections and hold them accountable for making progress toward their goals.

♦ Learn to recognize your own defensive mechanisms. Realize that you are probably not being attacked. Too often, we hear something other than what is being said or meant. We need to recognize our own hot buttons and learn to control them.

♦ When you catch yourself feeling defensive, don't react too quickly. Count to 10. Tell the other party that you can't discuss the issue right now—that you need some time to think about it. Try to avoid saying something on the spot that you'll regret later.

- Learn how to listen when someone asks a question or makes a suggestion. Get to the bottom of the question or request: Is there a bigger picture?

- Ask people to restate their question, comment, or suggestion. Doing so requires the asker to clarify the comment in his or her own mind, and it will give you time to think.

- Try to understand what others are saying by repeating what you think you heard.

- You may want to ask for more time to respond, then get back to the asker. This will give you time to work with the question, comment, or suggestion without the pressure of being on the spot.

- Consider that other people have good ideas that are just as valid as yours—they just may not present their ideas succinctly.

- Recognize that changing learned patterns of insecurity and defensiveness may take years of work.

 **Success Story: Understanding Others**

A school leader with many years and experiences under his belt believes that interpersonal skills are among the most important for effective leaders to develop and use. He has found that listening to and talking with others is critical to understanding reluctant followers. Many of the hesitant teachers, he said, "simply had different needs for information." He suggests that school leaders stop by individual teachers' rooms and talk to them one on one, which lets the defenses of both parties down. He invites challenges to his perceptions and doesn't take the challenges personally or make judgments. By asking teachers questions—asking them to open up and be reflective and honest and listening carefully—he is often able to identify the root of their concerns and allay their fears. Leaders need to be open to many perspectives, regardless of how much they disagree. "The principal must be seen as someone who is clear about their own values and ethics but respects others." With such a collegial process, any cultural, gender, or other biases can be acknowledged and worked through. Although they are time consuming to conduct, these one-on-one meetings will save time during larger staff meetings. Teachers can vent their frustrations and concerns in a less public arena and feel as if the leader has listened carefully.

This principal believes that an open and participatory leadership climate is critical. He worries about schools in which a clique of only a few people make decisions about the future direction of the school. "I've found that one of the most important things a principal can do is identify problems, pose questions, and then engage others in the process of seeking solutions. It is when the principal identifies the problem and the solution that they get more reluctance from the staff." Therefore, it is advisable to focus on results rather than methods, a theme that all of the principals interviewed identified. The methods are up for professional debate, but we all must agree on a well-defined and well-understood end. Clarity in the vision is essential. Again, it is the clear articulation and acceptance of the vision that seems to affect the success of any school initiative.

Part of a leader's job is to gather the resources necessary to make a decision or implement an agreed-upon plan of action. According to this principal, "Most people don't resist just to resist. They resist because they aren't sure they will be supported with training and other resources when they move to adopt new practices." Most teachers see themselves as successful in the present but have difficulty envisioning themselves as successful using new techniques and attitudes. They need to feel comfortable with the new ways in the same manner that the old ways provided familiarity.

Finally, this principal believes in establishing norms for decision making right from the beginning rather than waiting for conflict to arise. How do decisions get made? What does consensus mean? An agreed-upon "rule book" for decision making will help reduce arguments down the line. He noted, "Too often, groups wait until it's time to decide before deciding how to decide." (Interview with Ron Williamson, 2006.)[1]

## Summary

The determination of personality types and core beliefs goes a long way toward good communication. Listening to followers helps leaders develop professional relationships that lead to collaboration. Followers value leaders who strive to understand them and incorporate their perspectives. Effective leaders assess personality and learning styles and use them effectively to build teams of collaborative professionals.

## Resources

Gardner, H. (1983). *Frames of mind: The theory of multiple intelligences*. New York: Basic Books.

Goleman, D. (1998). *Working with emotional intelligence*. New York: Bantam Books.

Human Metrics. (n.d.). *Jung typology test*. Retrieved November 20, 2006, from http://www.humanmetrics.com/cgi-win/JTypes2.asp.

Institute for Management Excellence. (1999, March). *Dealing with difficult people*. Retrieved November 20, 2006, from http://www.itstime.com/mar99.htm.

Keirsey, D. (1998). *Please understand me II: Temperament, character, intelligence.* Del Mar, CA: Prometheus Nemesis.

Lopez-Campillo, J. (n.d.). *Cultural differences in the workplace: Stereotypes vs. sensitivity.* Retrieved November 20, 2006, from http://www.laborlawyers.com/CM/Seminar%20Materials/seminar%20materiala548.asp.

Williamson, R. (2006, August). Interview with the author.

[1]Ron Williamson is currently a member of the Educational Leadership Department at Eastern Michigan University.

# 4

# Defining Leadership Characteristics and Their Impact on Reluctant Followers

The principal was trying to design strategies for building professional relationships with some of his disengaged staff members. He decided that his first step was to look at something that was within his immediate control: He analyzed his own attitudes, behaviors, and expectations.

**Lead** (*v*): to show the way by going before or along; to act as a guide; to conduct.

## Defining Leadership

If you ask teachers, principals, or other professionals who have assigned leaders, they will consistently mention several qualities that are necessary to facilitate their followership:

- ◆ They expect leaders to be present—in the building and on the job —and visible. They appreciate visits to the classroom—where the rubber meets the road.

- They expect leaders to define roles for each position—who does what, why, and when.

- They expect to be treated as professionals who have a stake in the outcomes in their school.

- They expect leaders to communicate with them in an attempt to understand their values, needs, talents, and goals.

When James M. Kouzes and Barry Z. Posner (2002) used the Leadership Practices Inventory to survey more than 75,000 people over 20 years, they asked which characteristics would prompt people to willingly follow a leader. They found honesty, the ability to be forward looking, competence, inspiration, intelligence, fair-mindedness, broad-mindedness, and supportiveness at the top of their list; we can assume that leaders who embody the opposite characteristics would inspire people to *not* follow them. Reluctant followers have usually experienced poor leadership in the past and have not had an opportunity to be a part of a collaborative process.

Reluctant followers who dare leaders to lead them may have different expectations and definitions of the role of the leader. Too many teachers define the principal's role as that of disciplinarian first and instructional leader second. If a student misbehaves in class, the expectation is that the principal will deal with the student so that the teacher does not have to. When 10 faculty groups were asked to name the job that consumed the most of their leader's time, they said, "going to meetings." When asked which job should be the most time consuming, they said, "working with students." A lack of communication and a lack of clarity of role responsibilities often creates reluctance among staff members. Because leaders interpret their job descriptions differently and have personal priorities, followers (including parents), teachers, and students are often not sure who does what.

Faculty members at all levels of education often do not see quality control of classes as their job and leave that task to the administration. They may expect that the leader is the boss and should make all the decisions. They may feel that the leader is paid more and should have to do more work. They often make up their own personal definitions of the role of the leader to fit their own needs.

Followers who have always been followers may not understand the concepts and skills of leadership. If faculty members have been "managed" and not led, they will be skeptical of collaborative leadership. Some may believe the leader not doing his or her job and consequently refuse to participate.

While managers control and facilitate what needs to be done, leaders initiate the development of a vision of what the organization can become. Principals need to be both good managers and good leaders. Unfortunately, one of the brutal realities in education is that it's difficult to get some of the saboteurs onboard. So, leaders need to learn to work with and/or around them.

Much of the leadership research and literature contrasts two very different approaches to leadership. One type can be described as "I am leader, you are the follower." Power is inherent in the position. The school faculty is expected to comply with administrator decisions. Another brand of leadership is "Let's determine our goal and collaborate to plan steps to reach it. I'm here to help you." Principals of the former tend to focus on the implementation of various educational components: teaching and curricular innovations (like block scheduling), evaluation of teachers and coverage of their content, and adoption of reform models. In contrast, collaborative leaders focus on the end, student learning. They work side-by-side with their constituents to determine and communicate what student learning looks like and how effective they are in fostering learning. They look at the context of the school—determining what works, what doesn't, and planning for a local and unique design of reform.

Leaders of this type model learning for their teachers and their students. They gather data, discuss, brainstorm solutions, support teacher action research, discuss, make mistakes, reflect, discuss, and so on. Much of the recent literature suggests a moral component to leadership as well (see, for example, Sergiovanni). That is, "let's figure out what is the right thing to do," rather than "we're going to do this now." A shared moral vision, such as "We think that all of our students need to make concrete progress toward our stated goals," allows the educational staff to assume responsibility for the welfare of the entire school community rather than concentrate only on their own teaching.

Compare that vision to one like "Raise test scores," which leaves individual teachers to "do their own thing." Where are you in this continuum from being in charge to allowing collaboration to occur? Does the task that you have at hand require one or the other approach? Can you articulate your particular leadership style and match it to the task that needs to be accomplished?

Many followers who dare leaders to lead understand the concept of management but not the role of the visionary. They want the principal to discipline students, not to establish a plan to change student behavior. They want the leader to spend time fixing every classroom problem instead of establishing programs whereby students can get help and teachers can learn how to help them.

How do effective leaders deal with reluctant followers? What characteristics can be developed to counteract the damaging effects of those who wish to sabotage the efforts being made? Fortunately, recent research can shed light on this dilemma. For decades, researchers have attempted to identify the characteristics that define effective leadership. And there are as many types of leadership as there are authors to write about them. To complicate matters, there are different kinds of leaders and different kinds of followers and different contexts in which to lead.

This chapter concentrates on leadership characteristics that motivate others. In order to be effective, it is important to assess your own leadership type, determine the traits of the teachers in your schools, and analyze the situation in order to be most effective in building a strong support base.

## Assessing Leadership Types

The first step toward becoming an effective leader of reluctant followers is to determine your own philosophy. Do you want your teachers to be loyal to you or to a vision? You can become a very effective leader by being charismatic and engaging. Teachers may want to follow you because they like you and trust you. But what happens when you're gone? Will your legacy fall by the wayside as well? Leaders who help others to be loyal to a vision—for example, "All of our students will perform at grade level or higher"—see their role as sharing the power for long-term improvement. But note, too, that in order for this approach to be successful, all constituencies must know and completely understand the vision. In this example, what exactly constitutes grade-level performance?

Second, we have to accept the fact that no single innovation—no quick fix —will solve all of our problems and ensure that all of our students learn. Transformation is a slow process. It will take a while to get all of our constituencies on board—and even more complicated and time consuming is the task of letting some people go. Reluctant followers must know that you accept the premise that change will evolve and that it will not occur overnight.

We cannot expect extraordinary results in one year's time. Instead, effective leaders continually assess the status and use those data to show slow, if not marked, improvement in student learning (or change the strategies if improvement is not evident according to the data). It is important, though, that all constituencies see the progress. This implies that data will be collected and shared. Many of our reluctant followers whine about the "educational pendulum," believing that if they just wait out the new innovation (or the new leader), things will eventually go back to normal. And you know what? They're right.

To convince some reluctant followers, it's important that they understand we're not merely implementing one more educational fad; rather, we are forever evolving as we learn and assess. We are implementing continual systemic change that will help all of our students to perform at grade level or higher. Some of our ideas will work, some will not. But if we change nothing, we actually move the organization backward. Thus, an effective leader understands his or her level of collaboration with faculty, parents, and the central office. It is not enough for leaders to see the progress made; all constituencies must be confident that things are going in the right direction and understand where the path is leading.

Third, communications have to be clear. The rumor mill cannot operate in an effective organization. It can lead to erroneous thinking and dangerous subversion. For example, one school district that was establishing a new middle school distributed buttons to everyone who was in the know. The buttons said, "Ask me about our new middle school." Community members were free to ask people wearing the buttons about the philosophy and intricacies of the new organization and felt confident that they were getting the real story. It's also important to define your terms. For example, a principal who was leading a curricular reform in his school offered opportunities for all interested parties to serve on committees and share their ideas and suggestions. However, he was clear right from the beginning that "having your say doesn't necessarily mean having your way." All people involved understood *from the beginning* that all ideas would be considered, but certainly not all of them could be implemented. Effective leaders know how to facilitate group interactions, a skill that is necessary to the process (see Chapter 6 for ideas). Therefore, effective leaders assess their own communication skills and procedures. What do you do to make sure that everyone is on the same page—that is, heading in the same direction?

Fourth, admit to and tell the truth. Several unsuccessful schools we've worked with show only their good sides. A few of these schools conducted needs assessments but then redid them when the results didn't show what the leaders wanted. It's nice to be optimistic, but a good dose of skepticism is not a bad thing. Jim Collins calls this "Confront the Brutal Facts (Yet Never Lose Faith)" (2001, p. 65). This is another reason that data analyses are so important. We have to confront the realities in order to address them.

Cassellius (2006) describes the leadership process used in Memphis middle schools using Collins's (2001) Level 5 leadership components. She reinforced the idea that effective leaders share successes and challenges and seek input from others.

Fifth, model learning and risk taking. Many reluctant followers whine, "Sure, it's easy for him or her to say—when's the last time he or she was in a classroom?" Oops, right again. Good educational leaders get into the classroom one way or another (perhaps by doing walk-throughs or substitute teaching for a day every now and then). Teachers should perceive that the leader is undergoing just as much change as the followers. No one knows it all; we all have a lot to learn. Even if we go to conferences and read the literature, we still must implement plans locally, which necessitates learning, reflecting, and risk taking. Again, the key is that the risks are calculated and based on data and research rather than intuition or jumping on a popular bandwagon.

In their research summary, Pamela S. Angelle and Vincent Anfara (2006) identify 11 principles that leaders must consider:

1. Voluntary participation in the improvement process
2. Emphasis on ongoing change and improvement rather than a specific program or innovation
3. Involvement of staff at all levels in collaborative planning, problem solving, and decision making
4. Ongoing staff development for all involved
5. Planned follow-up coaching and support in applying new knowledge and skills
6. Involvement and leadership of the principal
7. Networking and visitation across districts and schools
8. Allocation of funds and resources
9. Designation and recognition of model schools
10. External technical assistance and support
11. Criteria or standards for schools of excellence

Paul Hersey and Kenneth Blanchard (1984) suggest that leadership type is dependent on the situation, including the developmental level of the teachers regarding a specific task. Low-level tasks in which teachers lack expertise can be accomplished by *telling* the teachers what to do and how to do it—for example, "This is how you are to record your grades using the new software." A more *consulting* form of leadership can be used when teachers are able to offer suggestions, but the principal still must direct the task—as in, "We're going to have parent conferences soon, how do you think we should organize the day?" *Participating* is a type of leadership that is highly supportive of teachers but low on the directives: "Let's work together to make our school inviting and exciting. How can we do that?" Finally, *delegating* is used when teachers assume full responsibility for the task—for example, "You have a schedule that lists only times when your kids go to specials; you figure out how to arrange your block of academic time." Professional learning communities and distributive leadership models, described in Chapter 7, take advantage of collaborative leadership to build ownership among stakeholders.

Problems occur when teachers and the principal see the task differently or when teachers do not value the goal. For example, if a teacher does not believe that school should be an inviting and exciting place but instead should be rigorous and directive, simply participating in the decisions will not result in any movement toward the goal. Therefore, it's important to understand that teachers must share in the vision. As we move into an era of greater collaboration, it's important to understand the developmental levels and philosophies of the teachers, parents, and community members.

Try to answer the following questions:

◆ What are your shared visions?

◆ Where do you have common ground?

◆ If your goal is that "All kids will perform at grade level," what does "grade level" mean?

◆ Can your goals be clarified so that everyone knows if and when you will get there?

Long-term systemic change in a school requires the collaboration of the entire school community toward a shared and distinct vision. Instead of focusing on what teachers do, we must focus on what it takes to ensure that our kids are learning.

Tests scores become a secondary focus; genuine learning is the primary focus. If learning occurs for all of our students—if they really are performing at grade level—then test scores will improve as a consequence. This approach counteracts the argument that "We can't implement X, we just have to meet our adequate yearly progress." If what we are doing now isn't helping all of our students perform at grade level or higher, then our moral duty is to figure out what we must do differently.

## Assessing Leadership Development

To move toward a collaborative approach, try to assess your own development. Determine where you fit in the continuum (this is not an either/or choice but a point along the continuum) on the next page.

Once leadership predilections are identified, the situation can be analyzed to determine which style is best suited to a specific challenge.

### Confronter Versus Mentor

A confrontational style describes a leader who sees problems or challenges and tells teachers to fix them. Often, even if only a few teachers are causing a problem (e.g., breaking a school rule by allowing students to chew gum), the confronter will make a blanket statement at a faculty meeting about making sure no kids chew gum. A mentor, on the other hand, will ask teachers who are allowing students to chew gum about their reasons for doing so.

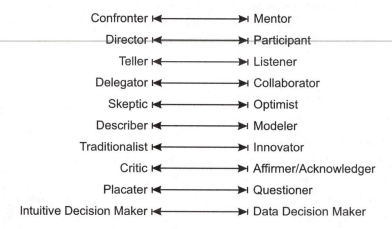

| Confronter | ←————————→ | Mentor |
| Director | ←————————→ | Participant |
| Teller | ←————————→ | Listener |
| Delegator | ←————————→ | Collaborator |
| Skeptic | ←————————→ | Optimist |
| Describer | ←————————→ | Modeler |
| Traditionalist | ←————————→ | Innovator |
| Critic | ←————————→ | Affirmer/Acknowledger |
| Placater | ←————————→ | Questioner |
| Intuitive Decision Maker | ←————————→ | Data Decision Maker |

### Director Versus Participant

A director knows what he or she wants to accomplish and tells others what to do (and sometimes how to accomplish it): "We're going to block scheduling. Here's what I want each of you to do." A participant, on the other hand, will ask a question—"How do we ensure that the kids' school time is used effectively?"—and collaborate to find ways to study and solve the problem Most participant-style leaders encourage action research in their schools rather than choose a popular component to implement. Participant leaders focus on student learning, along with the teachers and parents. There is a difference between an *instructional* leader and a *learning* leader (see, e.g., Eaker, DuFour, & Burnette, 2002).

### Teller Versus Listener

Many reluctant followers just can't tolerate being told what to do. They are the master of their own universe. Tellers tend to rile these followers, who will balk at the task *despite its value*. Listeners, however, find out what is motivating a teacher to act a certain way or use specific approach. They make sure they understand by rephrasing a teacher's statement for clarification or asking whether they have gotten the gist of it. Listeners are more apt to want constituents to have ownership of their learning. Tellers generally decide what's best and direct other people to implement it. Listeners ask a lot of questions to get to the root of the problem. They work hard at understanding those with whom they work.

### Delegator Versus Collaborator

Delegators are confident in the delegate's ability to accomplish a task without supervision, so the number of people with responsibility is limited to a few self-starters. Collaborators immerse themselves in the culture of the school and know the strengths and weaknesses of those around them. Collaborators help to study a particular challenge and seek input from the school community. The culture of the collaborative school is one of inquiry and reflection. Groups of professionals work to identify gaps in student learning and design ways to fill those gaps. Remember that the group is smarter than the individual, but many adults do not know how to work effectively in a collaborative setting. Teamwork isn't an accident—it takes work and leadership. "We cannot assume that a good faculty, even a good, *congenial* faculty, will work well together without a continued direction and support from the leadership within the school" (Hoerr, 2005, p. 111).

## Skeptic Versus Optimist

There's nothing wrong with a healthy dose of skepticism, but research tells us that we work only toward goals that we believe to be achievable. Skeptics doubt the ability of others without really finding out. Optimists, however, exude the sentiment that what we do makes a difference—but they back it up with real evidence. The tone of a school must be upbeat and optimistic. Optimism needs to be modeled for students. There needs to be a sense that "we do hard work here, but we have support from others and can be successful."

## Describer Versus Modeler

Modelers walk the talk. They model learning and changing. Leaders who are modelers show that they may not know all the answers, but they are willing to dive in to find out. Modelers are usually collaborators as well. Describers tend to be delegators: "I'll describe what needs to be done, then you do it." Part of the problem with this approach is that most people will do it their own way, which leads to a disconnect between the describer and the doer.

## Traditionalist Versus Innovator

Traditionalists focus on telling teachers what to do. They try to "fix" instruction. Innovators, on the other hand, focus on student learning and ask questions that lead to new approaches that directly affect student learning. Innovators don't just put in "things" that have been lauded in the professional literature. Rather, they and their colleagues look at specific data about student learning and come up with ways to assist their own students in their own school. Innovators take time to read the educational research and literature and reflect with others about its value locally.

## Critic Versus Affirmer/Acknowledger

Motivation theory tells us that we need to do challenging and meaningful work in order to stay motivated and that we need to believe that we can succeed. We also need to know that we're on the right track. It's not necessarily rewards that we need but acknowledgement for our hard work. In an innovative school, not all of our efforts will work. If a teacher takes a professional risk—one grounded in data, educational theory, and logic—then he or she needs to know that it will be alright if the innovation doesn't work as intended.

Many reluctant followers do not try because they fear public failure. If we want students to take academic risks, we need to model risk taking without fear of criticism. In this process, we are affirmed for our thoughtful approach but then assisted in studying what went wrong and how to fix it.

### Placater Versus Questioner

Too often, we try to suppress conflict. But conflict can be good. We need people to question our modus operandi and get us to move away from the status quo. In the the civil rights movement Dr. King rallied the troops and asked tough questions that most people didn't want to consider.

But if we don't admit that our present circumstances are flawed, we will never be able to convince our constituents that they should take a risk on something new. We have to admit that our society is quite different from that of the 1950s, yet we seem to want to continue to teach children of that time. Let's admit that we are not doing a good enough job in meeting the educational needs of *all* children.

### Intuitive Decision Maker Versus Data Decision Maker

We can study all kinds of research on the characteristics of effective leaders, but it comes down to this: Leaders cannot do it alone. Classrooms are the place where the rubber meets the road, and teachers are in control of the classroom. So without a doubt, the most significant characteristic of an effective leader is the ability to motivate and sustain motivation in every classroom for the benefit of every child's learning. To that end, leaders must understand the eccentricities of each teacher and know how to nurture each one. By "nurture," we do not mean to support blindly. Good leaders, including good parents, need to gently set parameters and expectations.

Chapter 3 described temperament theory and how to get good information that will help you lead teachers with different styles. Data analyses enable leaders to understand a challenge from the beginning. In the past, we implemented changes in our school delivery system because they were popular. Reluctant teachers do not stand for such an approach. Effective leaders show what is wrong and to what extent. They are questioners, inquirers. They collaborate to build a program on facts rather than popular opinions.

# Culture of the School

Every leader inherits a culture within an organization. Culture is what makes working in one school a different experience from another in a similar school organization. That culture may be positive, negative, or neutral. Positive cultures are easy to observe because employees have a common mission and a set of goals that everyone understands. There are formal and informal communication vehicles that give people timely and accurate information. People who work in an organization with a positive culture share success and a respect for the future.

Other organizations develop a culture that is fragmented, unfocused, and negative. The people within the organization do not participate in planning and do the minimum that is required to keep their jobs. In these organizations, the leader is expected to break from the status quo, bringing the constituencies along for the ride.

An effective leader analyzes the culture to determine what is important to the school community and what rites are valued. A leader who ignores the entrenched culture wastes valuable time and effort fighting the norms rather than making meaningful change occur. It is also important to remember that the leader is often not privy to the underlying culture. Many of the conversations that illustrate the school culture take place in the faculty room or hallways and stop when the leader enters.

The prevailing culture steers the attitudes and behaviors of those within the institution. Teachers act a certain way; students act a certain way. Behaviors do not change easily just because of a leader. New strategies must fit into the old culture, subtly causing the culture to shift. For example, if a school has a culture that says, "These are my kids, this is my room," it will be difficult to instill a sense of ownership for and by all.

Teaming, for example, will be difficult in such a culture because it doesn't fit in with the existing culture of isolation. Faculty members will exhibit behaviors that sabotage the cooperative efforts implied by teaming. It's so important, then, for the leader to observe, listen, and ask questions to determine the culture of the school. What does the faculty value? How can new changes be rooted in the already prevailing culture?

In the teaming example, starting with a cooperatively designed communications system may be the mechanism that is needed to start the cultural shift toward collaboration. The mechanism is nonthreatening, and most people will accept the fact that communications need to work well for the health of the institution and the people working in it. Therefore, the leader must ask:

♦ What do we value as a school community?

♦ How do we show our values?

- Is school a positive experience for those working in it—adults as well as students?
- What adds to this positive experience? What detracts from it? How can we change the detractions?
- What challenges do we have? What strategies have we used to surmount them? Did they work? If they are still challenges, then what else can we try?

Countless schools end up spending much of their time working on the fringes of culture rather than meeting it head on. For example, so many faculty meetings are spent discussing trivial concerns such as gum chewing. Is gum chewing really the issue, or is it entrenched in something bigger: What is the philosophy of behavior in this school community? Who's responsible? What message do we want to send to the students and their families? If we focus on the bigger questions, the trivial ones will fall into place.

To help define the school culture, try asking the following questions:

- What is our mission, purpose, or vision? What is unique about it? Is it used, or is it gathering dust in teachers' desk drawers? If it is used, who uses it? To what end?
- How do we know if we're making progress?
- What are our challenges? Which aspects can we control?
- How is this school community different than it was 10 years ago? Have we responded to change? How? What has worked? What hasn't? How do we know?
- What changes do we predict for the future? How can we be proactive in meeting changing needs?
- Think about the school culture (the visible and the submerged): What are we happy with? Why? What should we change? How can we change?

## Becoming a Reflective Professional

The literature on reflection can help us tackle the force of a school culture and help educational community members become problem solvers and active inquirers. Reflection can help us forgo the routine and examine our work in a thoughtful way, considering the context and different perspectives. Teachers are encouraged to look at their classroom from the students' perspective. Likewise, principals should examine their work through the eyes of teachers or parents. Good reflectors look at their work and determine how it could have gone better: What were the results of the lesson? Did all of the students learn? How do I know? If I were to do this lesson again, what would I do differently?

To establish a culture of reflection, a leader should model it. The leader should openly discuss the moral and ethical aspects of a decision, analyze its pros and cons, and steer future decisions in a way that connects the old with the new knowledge about learning in this school.

## Success Story: Starting Over

At the final faculty meeting before the holiday break, the principal, who was moving to a new building, identified 10 faculty members that he was taking with him. The assistant principal, who was taking over as principal after the holidays, was left with a faculty feeling very let down. They were not the chosen ones, and promises had been made and not kept. Her immediate job was to improve the self-esteem of these people and set a new tone.

Her first faculty meeting was called the inauguration of the "new" school, and it was quite different from what had happened in the past. There was a lot of food and a photographer to take pictures of the staff of the new school. It was a celebration of their "new" school. She gave the faculty her goals for the remainder of the year (her inaugural address):

◆ Survive and be smiling at the end of the year

◆ Prove that we have the best students

She built her support base by inviting the strongest teachers, whom she knew she could depend on, to join her in goal setting. With those people on board, she had a majority who could invite those who were reluctant to join them. She built on this strength by using that team of 12 to share ideas and make decisions. The support base was a cross-section of core, encore (specials), counselor, and other support personnel.

The support group was a conduit to the rest of the faculty. At the beginning of the second year, she selected teachers to sit in on the interview teams for hiring new faculty. They learned from the experience and defined a culture of their own while talking about what they were looking for in a faculty member. They asked, what must this person bring to our school? What do we most care about?

Many changes occurred during the second year in scheduling, teaming, and conferencing. Using the staff was a way to build support in the community, the school moved parent conferences from the afternoon to the evening to accommodate working parents. The staff's trade-off was a final afternoon free of conferences. For the first time, teams scheduled students instead of the counselors. This increased the flexibility of their scheduling.

Every faculty meeting was a professional development experience, free of "administrivia" and announcements. Those were sent in the weekly and daily announcements, so faculty members were free to concentrate on professional development at the meetings. Weekly press releases were sent to the community.

The principal was able to overcome reluctance by releasing an ineffective teacher who had been rewarded in the past by having less to do. The message coming across to the faculty was this: If you are really bad, you do not have to teach. Realizing that everyone in the building was expected to be a fully participating professional, the faculty began to hold higher expectations for themselves.

The strategies that this leader used in her second year were based on the knowledge that teachers strengthen each other through relationships, rituals, and establishment of their own group culture. She made it very uncomfortable for teachers who were not team players. She identified reluctant staff members as teachers who

- Did not want to change
- Did not want to work hard
- Were not sure of themselves
- Did not like kids
- Lacked spontaneity and were boring in their teaching
- Felt that teaching was just a job

Her leadership style included a great deal of modeling behavior as she demonstrated different ways to teach the same material. As the school revised its advisory program, she had many reluctant teachers. She carefully selected people for the committee, including staff members who were reluctant. They were invited by others to be a part of the process. Once they were invited to be a part of the decision-making process, they gave up their reluctance.

At the end of the school year, the sixth grade had always gone to an outdoor education program for a week, but the sixth grade teachers did not go. Most of the teachers who were going were seventh-grade teachers. The leader formed a committee to discuss the pros and cons of this model and decided that it was more beneficial to have teachers who were currently teaching the students attend the outdoor education program. One reluctant teacher on the committee got very involved in the scheduling, planning, and curriculum because she would now be teaching her own students.

When this principal moved to open a new building, she used both her former strategies and some new ones:

- She started a buddy system among the teachers, pairing them for specific tasks with another teacher in a different team or grade.

This improved the communication and climate in the entire building.

- She spent time developing relationships with people and treated them well. She made recognition of staff a priority and did not ask teachers to do anything she would not do herself.
- She held student lock-ins (for all three grades) at the school to get the students to bond. All teachers had to give up 24 hours for the lock-in, but in return, she gave them a morning off of their choice. She was at every lock-in with the staff and students.

This leader set her goals to win over reluctant people and believes that personalization was important to her success.

When asked which skills a new school leader most needs, she offered the following:

- Personality—Be able to work with all people. You have to constantly work on being a people person.
- Patience—It takes time to turn things around. You have to know where people are starting from.
- Planning—Have a vision and plan it out. Share goals and leave them open-ended so that staff can have input. Ask the staff how they see the plan developing.
- Watch out for the personal welfare of teachers. Be aware of their basic needs. Open the pop machine, feed them, and listen.

This leader was so successful in her first two schools that she was sought out in another state to open a model school. Her skills in working with reluctant staff and her leadership qualities have been lauded and applauded by hundreds of other leaders as she and her staff have made presentations at national conferences. The bottom line is that she and her staff made a significant difference in the achievement of the students in her buildings. Today, she is a consultant to principals in the Union Pacific Railroad Foundation, sponsored Principals' Project (see www.principalspartnership.org).
(Interview with Marion Payne, 2006.)[1]

## Summary

Leadership styles and characteristics have a significant impact on the attitudes of followers. The culture of the school can be positive, negative, or neutral. An effective leader understands the culture, the underlying values, and the people who work within that culture. The leader must constantly listen, observe, and ask questions to determine the current culture of the school. Leaders who are effective with reluctant followers know their own philosophy and leadership style, and they know that change takes time. Leaders cannot effect change by themselves. The most significant characteristic of an effective school leader is the ability to motivate and sustain motivation in every classroom for the benefit of every child's learning.

## Resources

Angelle, P. S., & Anfara, V. (2006). Courageous, collaborative leaders confront the challenges and complexities of school improvement. *Middle School Journal, 37*(5), 48–54.

Cassellius, B. (2006). Using relationships, responsibility, and respect to get from "good to great" in Memphis middle schools. *Middle School Journal, 37*(5), 4–15.

ChangingMinds.Org. (2003). *The leader-follower loop.* Retrieved November 27, 2006, from http://changingminds.org/disciplines/leadership/followership/follower_loop.htm.

Collins, J. C. (2001). *Good to great: Why some companies make the leap—and others don't.* New York: HarperBusiness.

Earker, R. Dufour, R., & Burnette, R. (2002). *Getting started: Restructuring schools to become professional learning communities.* Bloomington, IN: National Educational Service.

Hersey, P., & Blanchard, K. (1984). *A situational approach to managing people.* Escondido, CA: Blanchard Training and Development.

Hoerr, T. R. (2005). *The art of school leadership.* Alexandria, VA: Association for Supervision and Curriculum Development.

Kouzes, J. M., & Posner, B. Z. (2002). *History of leadership research.* Retrieved November 27, 2006, from http://www.sedl.org/change/leadership/history.html.

Marzano, R. J., Waters, T., & McNulty, B. A. (2006). *School leadership that works: From research to results.* Alexandria, VA: Association for Supervision and Curriculum Development.

Payne, M. (2006, August). Interview with the author.

Reeves, D. B. (2006). *The learning leader: How to focus school improvement for better results.* Alexandria, VA: Association for Supervision and Curriculum Development.

Scott, B. (2006, August). Interview with the author.

Sergiovanni, T. J. (2006). *The principalship: A reflective practice perspective* (5th ed.). Boston: Pearson/Allyn & Bacon.

[1]Marion Payne is currently a consultant to the Union Pacific Principals Partnership. www.principalspartnership.com

# 5

# Motivating
# Reluctant Followers

The principal was new to the school. She was excited about joining a school with a mature faculty in a school that was doing well. She figured this would be a faculty of enthusiastic instructional leaders. Unfortunately, what she found was a group of complacent teachers who held an "if it ain't broke, don't fix it" attitude. She couldn't motivate them to try anything new.

How do you eat an elephant? One bite at a time. The attitudes and behaviors of teachers are set over a long period of time, and it will usually take a while for an optimistic leader to turn things around. The stubbornness and lack of enthusiasm have probably been accepted (or at least tolerated) in the past and have provided some benefits to the teachers—which is why such behaviors have become so ingrained and have been able to flourish. The key is to set high and clear expectations, face the situation personally and head on, remain patient, and stay optimistic.

Think about motivation in any given situation. Motivation is inspired by interest, choice, perceived value of the task, and ownership of the situation. In the traditional school organization, the central office dictates to the building administrators, who dictate to the teachers, who dictate to the students. In such an organization, only the decision makers at the top have investment in the task. The values and priorities of the teachers are often compromised in such an organization, and teachers feel powerless. These feelings of powerlessness often lead to disgruntled attitudes at best and outright defiance at worst. As a result, many schools are now collapsing this hierarchy by instituting a professional learning community approach (Eaker, DuFour, & Burnette, 2002).

Alma Harris (2003) envisions a professional learning community as an organizational structure in which leaders and teachers as leaders share a vision, engage in collaborative problem solving and decision making, and assume joint responsibility for their work. This organization disperses school leadership and focuses on the end product—student achievement—rather than a particular task or instruction in general. The central tasks become the development of a collaborative, clear, engaging, and inspiring vision and the establishment of an environment that allows such collaboration to occur. For example, one effective principal defined her most important and difficult task as "making sure the alligators stay in the moat." She wanted to protect her school community in order to allow the school professionals to collaborate and make important decisions about their students' learning. Teachers become leaders and principals become the leaders of leaders in a professional learning community. Teachers can accurately describe themselves as change agents in the school. They make meaningful decisions that directly affect learning and achievement. Teachers who try to slide by anonymously suddenly find themselves in the thick of things, giving important input and making important decisions. Putting the "P" back in professional allows teachers to feel that they make a difference. Their ideas are sought after and valued. Professional development seminars become work, discussion, and research-sharing sessions about the challenges in their particular school. Talking heads lead in-service days only at the teachers' request.

To establish an organization that fosters teacher motivation, consider the following elements in transforming the school culture:

- A common set of values
- An inspiring shared vision with goals that focus directly and clearly on student learning (as opposed to instruction or test scores)
- Meaningful celebrations and rituals
- Inquiry and teacher reflection to foster professional dialogue on a regular basis
- A sense of true professionalism and professional development whereby teachers are recognized for their knowledge, skills, and efforts
- Collaboration

# Visions, Values, and Celebrations

As a school community, what do you hope to accomplish? Where can or should you be? What does your community value? What does your school value? Can you determine by looking at your school what is important to you? If a stranger came into your school and looked around the building, what information would he or she learn about the values of the school?

What do the teachers in the school value? What do they hope to accomplish? If the teachers' values and visions differ widely from the school leader's values and vision, conflict will surely occur. An effective leader won't try to impose his or her beliefs on a faculty but will determine the pre-existing priorities of the teachers. Often, the leader will discover that the faculty are stuck in the details and lack an achievable vision to unify the staff. To make any progress, the leader needs to facilitate professional dialogue about the purposes and aims of the school. Do not start by focusing on the difficulties but rather what end you strive toward.

The first step in fostering collaboration and a sense of school community is to establish your baseline. Everyone needs to believe in the philosophy of the school. All innovations, then, must advance that philosophy. When the philosophical bases are unclear, it's difficult to determine what fits and what doesn't. People feel free to do their own thing. It's challenging to stay motivated when you don't know what you're aiming at. Everyone should know the school's purpose and understand how it translates into daily life in the school. The vision drives the school, and everything done in the school serves its purpose. This implies that philosophical leanings are discussed and consensus is reached. The mission of the school is not set by a select few on a committee but is filtered through all of the stakeholders. A set of identified values builds a vision that can be articulated in the school's mission statement. (For more on writing an effective mission statement, see the Council on Middle Level Education, 1987). A vision, then, is future oriented: Given your mission, where do you want to go? Then decide how you're going to get there.

Rituals and celebrations refocus the school community on these values.

One school, for example, values communal support. So, it starts each day with a team meeting, designed and delivered by students, that sends a message of comradeship and caring. The impact of the meeting is profound. Its message is repeated throughout the course of the day. Teachers and students start every day with a mutual emphasis on school as community. During the meeting, individuals and groups are recognized for their efforts and successes. Students regularly thank teachers for their help during these meetings, and teachers recognize students for their efforts, perseverance, and achievements beyond the classroom walls. The meetings project a sense that "we're all here together doing hard and important work and we're all here to help one another succeed." Teachers, students, and administrators feel valued in that school. Impromptu collaborative problem solving is the norm.

Another school celebrates learning by showcasing student work. Community members and parents are invited to the school (through handwritten invitations from the students) to observe the work that students are mastering. A play might be performed in the auditorium while science and social studies projects are explained in the hallway and math problems are solved on a board in the lobby of the school. Adults share in the celebration of learning, and students enjoy a wider audience for their work, giving them a broader incentive to do well.

## Inquiry, Reflection, and Professionalism

One important way of bringing teachers on board is to base the school's decisions on real-life data. Instead of jumping on any popular bandwagon, effective leaders involve the school community in a local needs assessment. First, find out where you are whether you want to go somewhere else. Inquiry in the school will reveal strengths and challenges that need to be identified. Each person in the community should develop personal goals regarding what he or she can personally do to enhance the strengths and make progress toward overcoming the challenges. We can't assume that all teachers contribute the same skills to the workplace. Teachers and administrators should reflect on their own personal values and attributes and volunteer their efforts to help in a particular way. For example, one teacher may be a good researcher and can read up on what other successful schools have done; another teacher may be an effective contact with parents and the community; another may establish an organizational clearinghouse to make sense of all the data and resources collected. The point is that all professionals have important skills, abilities, and interests that are valuable to the professional team. When people feel that their efforts are valued and important, they are more motivated to contribute. If they are asked to tackle a task that is beyond the scope of their ability, they will usually decline the work or prevent the work from being accomplished. Self-efficacy theory tells us that motivation is determined by the degree to which a person feels he or she can succeed. If the task seems daunting or beyond a person's ability, he or she will often demean the task and describe it as a worthless enterprise. This behavior, referred to as *self-handicapping*, may include procrastination, purposeful lack of effort, and chronic complaint (see, e.g., Riggs, 1992; Urdan & Midgely, 2001). Such behavior should raise a red flag for the vigilant leader. It calls for one-on-one discussion to determine the basis for such reluctance and a goal-setting task that will help the teacher to participate in a nonthreatening yet helpful way.

Consistent reflection will help teachers define their strengths and weaknesses and give them a basis for professional decision making. Reflection in the education arena implies more than merely thinking about one's practice. It includes more than describing what occurred through the development of a personal voice and ownership of ideas. Practitioners who use reflection consider many different perspectives (especially the perspectives of students) and make ethical decisions. Effective reflectors set goals that are based on what they have learned about themselves and their practice with regard to the vision the school has established. "Reflection requires teachers to be introspective, open-minded, and willing to be responsible for decisions and actions" (Evans & Pollicella, 2000, p. 62).

## Collaboration

A leader certainly cannot achieve student learning alone. The classroom is where the rubber meets the road. Therefore, leaders and teacher-leaders need to collaborate and conspire for the welfare of all students. In such a school, for example, one student stated, "In this school, teachers talk about the kids. And it's good."

Effective leaders reinforce the vision of the school and communicate high expectations. Teachers do not feel that they can close their classroom door and go it alone. In collaborative schools, teachers consult one another, observe one another, and share educated opinions about professional literature and strategies. The faculty room is filled with discussions that are focused on possibilities rather than complaints. The leader of the school continues to remind the faculty of their commitment and ultimate responsibility—the achievement of each and every student in the school.

 **Success Story: Focus on Learning**

The school leader has tackled several different grade levels and school cultures. She works hard at developing a professional learning environment in which all adults and students are focused on learning. Every day, she begins by focusing on what is important, and she writes an e-mail message to the staff to help them do the same. It is apparent that she is well read; everyone takes her ideas seriously. She exudes confidence in those around her and displays an expectation that her faculty is focused on student learning and behavior. As you read over a few of her daily e-mails, notice that the language is consistent and the vision is clear.

This principal has been assigned to several troubled inner-city schools. She approaches the faculty as professionals and challenges them to follow her lead as a go-getter who constantly strives to make academic and behavioral strides in her school. She believes that all professionals need to be voracious readers of the literature and share what they have read, discuss it, and figure out how to implement new ideas that will make a difference. Every day, she writes an e-mail message to her faculty to remind them of their responsibilities and to refer them to resources that may help:

Happy first day of school! Wow! What an impressive week we had together! We were powerful in our learning and thinking during our PLC [professional learning community] time. We were warm and welcoming to families during Open House. Today we begin to make our visions reality through our actions with our students! Each morning I will send an e-mail to focus and refocus us on making our vision for McPhee students, families, and staff come alive then thrive!

### High Achieving Students—
### Work Hard, Get Smart! Work Harder, Get Smarter!

Today your students will know if you believe that they can learn, perform, and behave at grade level or above, (student efficacy). Your students will also know if you believe in yourself (personal efficacy)—your power and persistence to get them to grade level or above! Your actions, your words, your body language, your organization, your instruction, your high expectations, your caring relationships communicate what you believe. Your beliefs are the foundation of high achieving students! Our power as a school, (collective efficacy), will create the collaborative culture to solve the problems that none of us could solve alone!

### High-Achieving Staff—Focused on Learning—PLC

From *On Common Ground: The Power of Professional Learning Communities,* by DuFour, Eaker, and DuFour: "The right image to embrace of a professional learning community is a group of teachers who meet regularly to share, refine and assess the impact of lessons and strategies continuously to help increasing numbers of students learn at higher levels." Think of the work we have done already that embraces this definition of PLC. Think of the work we will do as we meet as grade-level teams, PLCs, and SAT teams. What a difference we will make in the life trajectory of our students!

### High-Achieving Schools—
### Raising All Achievement While Closing the Gaps

From *Closing the Achievement Gap: A Vision for Changing Beliefs and Practices,* by Belinda Williams: "Subscribing to a deficit model of cultural, parental, and community resources and values limits the allies educators believe they can call upon for support…If on the other hand, educators began with a belief in the transformative role of education, the value of accessing diversity, a faith in the potential success of every student, a commitment to collaborative and political linkages with parents and communities, then mustering the inventiveness to create new ways of organizing on behalf of children would be the logical, moral, and just thing to do." The logical, moral, and just thing to do: closing the achievement gap!

### BIST—Teach and Protect

Today begin teaching the processes of BIST [Behavior Intervention Support Team]. Practicing and role playing will ensure that there are no surprises for our kids. We also start building caring relationships (grace) and establishing high expectations (accountability) today!

### FISH! Catch the Energy and Release the Potential

(From the 2006 FISH! Calendar) "Choose Your Attitude: Imagine the life you could live if you choose to make your vision a reality. Choosing the attitude that reflects your vision is the first step in the journey."

Bess

\*\*\*\*\*\*\*\*\*\*\*\*\*\*\*\*\*\*\*\*\*\*\*\*\*\*\*\*\*\*\*\*\*\*\*\*\*\*\*\*\*\*\*\*\*\*\*\*\*\*\*\*\*\*\*\*\*\*\*\*\*\*\*\*\*\*\*

The Capitol Team: Together Everyone Achieves More!

\*\*\*\*\*\*\*\*\*\*\*\*\*\*\*\*\*\*\*\*\*\*\*\*\*\*\*\*\*\*\*\*\*\*\*\*\*\*\*\*\*\*\*\*\*\*\*\*\*\*\*\*\*\*\*\*\*\*\*\*\*\*\*\*\*\*\*

---

Good Morning!

### High-Achieving Students—
### Work Hard, Get Smart! Work Harder, Get Smarter!

Efficacy: 1. All adults believe that all children can learn, perform, and behave at grade level or above. Do you also realize embedded in this statement is our efficacy as educators? We must also believe that we have the power, knowledge, skill, desire to learn, and persistence to problem solve to take action to get all students to learn, perform, and behave at grade level or above. Simplified, we know we can do it! Remember our students' radar: not only can they sense what we believe about them, they also can "read" what we believe about ourselves!

### High-Achieving Staff—Focused on Learning—PLC

From *On Common Ground: The Power of Professional Learning Communities,* by DuFour, Eaker, and DuFour: The introduction reinforces the concept of student efficacy, educator efficacy and school (collective) efficacy. Do we "acknowledge our ability to impact student achievement and accept responsibility for creating an efficacious school?"

On a scale of 1–10, 10 being the highest level of efficacy, where are McPhee students? McPhee Staff? McPhee as a school? What actions do we need to take to reach a 10 for each group?

### High-Achieving Schools— Raising All Achievement While Closing the Gaps

From *Closing the Achievement Gap: A Vision for Changing Beliefs and Practices,* by Belinda Williams: Williams summarizes how this integration of theoretical knowledge will close the achievement gap. Our knowledge base will change from individual psychology to improve achievement to sociocultural development to close the achievement gap. Our focus of intervention will change from teaching (curriculum, instruction, and assessment) to improve achievement to learning (the learner and supports for learners) to close the achievement gap. Traditional strategies to increase achievement are working but they are not closing the gap. I know that we in LPS and we at McPhee can figure this out! (It's our soul's code.)

### BIST—Teach and Protect

If we are being consistent with early intervention and caring confrontation, our chronic students have already become quite visible. I think this makes us feel like BIST is not working when it is really an indication that we are holding all students accountable. If you have a student who already has three to five safe seats and/or buddy rooms, we need to figure out what their repetitive behavior is telling us. Are we getting to all five stages of accountability in our processing? Have we pulled out a protective plan form and started problem solving what a protective environment will be for this student? It's what we do after the safe seat that makes the difference and develops the three BIST life skills.

### FISH! Catch the Energy and Release the Potential

(From the 2006 FISH! Calendar) "FISH! Philosophy: The FISH! Philosophy may be simple, but that doesn't mean it's easy. On the contrary, among life's most challenging tasks are holding on to the spirit of play, living consciously, being generous with others, and taking responsibility for ourselves."

Bess

\*\*\*\*\*\*\*\*\*\*\*\*\*\*\*\*\*\*\*\*\*\*\*\*\*\*\*\*\*\*\*\*\*\*\*\*\*\*\*\*\*\*\*\*\*\*\*\*\*\*\*\*\*\*\*\*\*\*\*\*\*\*\*\*\*\*\*\*

The Capitol Team: Together Everyone Achieves More!

\*\*\*\*\*\*\*\*\*\*\*\*\*\*\*\*\*\*\*\*\*\*\*\*\*\*\*\*\*\*\*\*\*\*\*\*\*\*\*\*\*\*\*\*\*\*\*\*\*\*\*\*\*\*\*\*\*\*\*\*\*\*\*\*\*\*\*\*

As you can see, this effective leader lives and models her own philosophy and hard work for her staff and students. She works to help her faculty identify personal and professional goals and understand how they intersect or do

not intersect with the school's direction. She helps staff understand the lives they are trying to create and how school fits into what they are trying to create. When they know what they are trying to create, they either become less reluctant or they leave.
(Interview with Dr. Bess Scott, 2006.)[1]

## Summary

Motivational attitudes and habits can be changed—in students and in adults. Astute leaders do not merely accept the reluctant behaviors of the people with whom they work. Rather, they assess their own traits and those of their colleagues and charges. In a professional environment, an expectation of collegiality, collaboration, and collective ownership of responsibilities motivates adults and students to strive toward success and excellence. (Interview with Dr. Bess Scott, 2006.)*

## Resources

Behavior Intervention Support Team. (n.d.). *BIST in your school and community.* Retrieved November 27, 2006, from http://www.bist.org.

Council on Middle Level Education. (1987). *Developing a mission statement for the middle level school.* Reston, VA: National Association of Secondary School Principals.

DuFour, R., Eaker, R., & DuFour, R. (Eds.). (2005). *On common ground: The power of professional learning communities.* Bloomington, IN: Solution Tree.

Earker, R., DuFour, R., & Burnette, R. (2002). *Getting started: Reculturing schools to become professional learning communities.* Bloomington, IN: National Educational Service.

Efficacy Institute, Waltham, MA. http://www.efficacy.org.

Evans, J., & Pollicella, E. (2000). Changing and growing as teachers and learners: A shared journey. *Teacher Education Quarterly, 27*(3), 55–70.

Harris, A. (2003). Teacher leadership as distributed leadership: Heresy, fantasy, or possibility? *School Leadership and Management, 23,* 313–324.

Moyer, A. (2006). *Gauging the existing leadership effectiveness of middle school teacher team leaders for the formation of a professional learning community.* Unpublished doctoral dissertation, Immaculata University.

Riggs, J. (1992). Self-handicapping and achievement. In A. K. Boggiano & T. S. Pittman (Eds.), *Achievement and motivation: A social-developmental perspective.* New York: Cambridge University Press.

Sagor, R. (2003). *Motivating students and teachers in an era of standards.* Alexandria, VA: Association for Supervision and Curriculum Development.

Scott, B. (2006, August). Interview with the author, Lincoln, NE.

Urdan, T., & Midgley, C. (2001). Academic self-handicapping: What we know, what more there is to learn. *Educational Psychology Review, 13*(2), 115–138.

Williams, B. (Ed.). (2003). *Closing the achievement gap: A vision for changing beliefs and practices.* Alexandria, VA: Association for Supervision and Curriculum Development.

[1]Dr. Bess Scott is currently the principal at the McPhee Elementary School in Lincoln, Nebraska.

# 6

# Minimizing the Dare: Strategies for Communicating With Reluctant Followers

Progress was slow for the new administrator in the high school. The goals she had set in the summer were still not even started, and she was barely maintaining the status quo. She had told the faculty that they needed to revise the way they did conferences, but nothing had been done. This was to be the meeting at which everyone would hear what she had planned. Attendance was poor, with fewer than half of the group present. Those who were there had come to protect the status quo. Her enthusiasm had been misinterpreted as decree and created a large number of reluctant followers.

They were very surprised when she immediately put them into groups and asked them to brainstorm ways they could improve the current conferencing system. When the groups shared, there were many good new ideas. She then asked them to rank those that they thought could be implemented within the current school year, and there were several.

She then asked for volunteers to meet with her the next day to determine how to get these ideas communicated to the rest of the faculty.

She had diminished reluctance by using group involvement and communication plans. She decided to facilitate more communication among the faculty, and they decided that perhaps she had some good ideas that would help the students.

To gain followers and keep a group working productively, leaders must always remember to bring along the MICE.

*Motivation:* What is the goal to be accomplished?

*Inclusion:* How can I involve everyone?

*Communication:* What system do I need to implement to make sure that everyone has the information?

*Evaluation:* How will I know whether the process is working?

Because motivation was discussed in the previous chapter, this chapter focuses on the rest of the MICE—strategies for including everyone in the process, communication systems and strategies, and evaluation of the process.

# Inclusion

### Strategy 1: Establish a Leader's Advisory Council

The purpose of this strategy is communication, but a larger purpose is to build a coalition of leaders who are pursuing the same vision. Most of the leaders interviewed for this book said that they use an advisory council for discussion, goal setting, and communication. The membership rotates so that many people are participants during the school year. All participants have to be elected or appointed by their peers. This advisory council is made up of teachers, parents, and students. During council meetings, the leader's job is to listen to concerns and issues and take suggestions for improvement. Reluctant followers are more likely to speak up when they are given a legitimate forum in which to express their concerns.

### Strategy 2: Define the Belief System and Bottom Line

Establish your own goals for the present and future, but then discuss them and have all affected people give input, make additions, and make adjustments. If possible, do goal setting with the group. "Large scale reform requires pluralized leadership, with teams of people creating and driving a clear coherent strategy…The moral imperative means that everyone has a responsibility for changing the larger educational context for the better" (Fullan, Bertani, & Quinn, 2004, p. 3). Reluctant followers respond best to a well-developed plan of action with purpose statements for the process and products. For example, one principal has all the goals printed and posted in the halls for everyone to see. Teachers, students, parents, and the community are constantly reminded of what the school's goals.

### Strategy 3: Hold One-on-One Conferences With Each Faculty or Group Member Before School Starts

These conferences are only 10 minutes in length but cover goal setting and personal concerns that staff members may have. The purpose is to assure all followers that you are willing to listen. The time spent on these is insurance against personnel problems that may occur later in the year.

### Strategy 4: Give Group Members a Brief Written Survey to Express Their Ideas and Concerns

This is especially effective if the survey can be answered by e-mail. All faculty surveys should be no more than five questions. For example, one principal has a survey question of the week in every bulletin that goes to staff, students, and parents, and the results are published the following week. Sample questions include the following: How do you think we should reward students who have been great citizens in our school? How can we improve the health of all people who come to this building? What extracurricular activities can we offer to include more students?

### Strategy 5: Let the Majority Be Heard

Too often, reluctant followers have louder voices or are more intimidating than the majority of staff who support a person or idea. When the majority has a voice and is recognized by the leadership, this keeps the group of reluctant followers from growing in size and status.

### Strategy 6: Give Reluctant Followers Responsibility for Activities From Which They Can Gain Positive Status

"The goal is to have the teacher do something so you can offer thanks and recognition for efforts when the goal is accomplished. Building a feeling self-value is an essential part of making a difficult teacher (group member) feel like a contributing member of the school" (Whitaker, 2002, p. 136). Provide as much information as possible to show that the change will be safe to implement, and offer resources to form collaborative groups with others who have been successful.

### Strategy 7: Be Sensitive to the Emotional Response to Change When Including People in the Process

Most reluctant participants say they are reluctant because they do not know what their new role will be. This response can be especially prevalent when schools adopt teaming and peer coaching. Many people who have been quite comfortable teaching on their own suddenly have their teaching styles and problems illuminated for their colleagues to see.

## Strategy 8: Assess What Is Needed to Support the Skill Development of Personnel

Reluctant personnel are not sure what skills are required to do what is expected of them. Leaders must articulate the responsibilities and competencies needed for the change and then provide the necessary training. How many school personnel now know 10 times more about technology than they did two years ago? Most do because they have had training in using technology in the classroom.

## Strategy 9: Offer a Pilot Program to Evaluate New Tasks Before Implementing a Program

Many who have been successful with school change have brought reluctant followers along by calling the first phase of the change process a pilot program. This strategy places everyone on the team or group on an even playing field and implies that the process can be changed as people try it. Some leaders allow teachers to volunteer for the pilot program and have others observe.

For example, Waukeegan High School in Illinois wanted to offer an alternate ninth-grade program using teaming and an integrated curriculum. Many teachers were skeptical, but everyone was invited to participate. Six teachers volunteered during the first year, and their activities, teaming, and curriculum was closely watched by the rest of the staff. Because of their success and enthusiasm, another team was added to the ninth grade during the second year, and a sophomore team was started. Those who were extremely reluctant were allowed to continue using the traditional model, but they were encouraged to make curriculum changes.

## Strategy 10: Include Everyone in the Communication

Too often, when a change is anticipated, rumors and pieces of information will cause undue anxiety among those who will be asked to implement the change. When followers do not consider themselves a part of the inner circle of decision making, they listen to this information and often do not ask for the whole model. This leads to more dissent than is necessary.

Often, reluctant followers only know a bit of information, and from that, they make erroneous assumptions. They have their own perceptions and views that are narrow or wrong. Reluctance develops when a follower does not see how he or she fits into the total picture. Thus, leaders not only must communicate with all followers but also must find ways to include them in the group process. If leaders want groups to function fully as decision makers, they must be sure that

- All members know the purpose of the change.
- All members know where and when the group is meeting.
- All members know their role in the group.
- All members know how to communicate with the leader and other group members.

## Data Gathering

Data can show reluctant followers exactly what students do all day in school. Shadow studies, for example, are an effective way to communicate the expectations that a student receives during a single day. During a shadow study, a teacher follows a randomly selected student's schedule for an entire day and logs what the expectations are, what the class is doing, and how the student is responding every three to five minutes. From this activity, a snapshot of the life of a typical student emerges. This data, when shared with the faculty, can become a powerful catalyst for discussion about the impact that a school day has on students (Lounsbury & Johnston, 1985).

One high school principal keeps a large whiteboard in the faculty meeting area and asks every teacher to post their assignments for each grade level for the week. Projects and programs are also listed so that everyone can see what is expected of a typical freshman, sophomore, junior, or senior during the week. This visual illustration of student expectations created a type of faculty discussion that had not been present in the school before. Teachers could begin to see why some students were having difficulty getting their work done. Leading the faculty through the problem of failing students became easier for this principal, who helped them provide their own descriptive data of the problem.

Teaching teams that create homework calendars for students have more success getting the work completed. Talking about homework requires faculty members to communicate with each other to solve a problem. Someone must lead them to the solution to this and other problems. Communication issues that affect everyone in the school system, such as homework, grades, and conferences, are like snowballs teetering atop a snowy mountain. Left unattended, they will roll downhill and become large boulders blocking your path.

Many of these problems can be solved with an accurate communication system that includes local data.

# Communication

Although there are literally hundreds of communication strategies, those used with reluctant followers require that the leader first be able to listen to the reluctance. Every person interviewed for this book cited their ability to listen as the main ingredient in their success with reluctant followers. They did not say *agree,* they said *listen.* That tactic is a part of all of the strategies listed here. It is implied in every conversation.

## Strategy 11: Every Organization Needs a Written Communication System

People need to know

◆ Who makes decisions

◆ Who answers questions

◆ Where to go for help

◆ How to communicate with personnel

◆ When people are available

A lack of information creates resistance, reluctance, and apathy.

When students are in elementary school, parents typically deal with only one teacher and principal. As these students move into middle school, parents may interact with a team, a counselor, a school secretary, an assistant principal, a principal, and an adviser. Parents often wonder who does what and how they can get information. As these students move into high school, there will be six to eight teachers who probably do not function as a team, a counselor, a coach, an attendance secretary, an assistant principal, and a principal. In addition, many parents think they should call the superintendent's office if they have a problem unless a written communication is given to them telling them who to call.

If the system is not clearly articulated to those who work in it and are clients of it, leadership will spend a great deal of their energy answering questions that should have gone to someone else. The lack of a clearly defined system also creates mistrust in followers, as they believe there is an inner circle of people who know what is going on and make the real decisions, whereas they are only asked for input after decisions are made.

Interviews with successful leaders, research, and observation have all been used to create the strategies given here. Most of the strategies are proactive and intended to keep reluctant followers from becoming reluctant in the first place.

## Strategy 12: Create a Visual Communication Document

In the visual communication document, indicate who does what, when they are available, and how to contact them. Look at the following networks that exist in most schools and make sure they are included:

- ◆ All personnel to administration
- ◆ Administration to all personnel
- ◆ Administration to parents and students
- ◆ Students and parents to administration
- ◆ Teachers to teachers
- ◆ Teachers to counselors and specialists
- ◆ Counselors and specialists to teachers
- ◆ Teachers to parents
- ◆ Parents to teachers, counselors, and specialists
- ◆ Students to parents
- ◆ Parents to students
- ◆ Students to students

This chart or document is usually written in the student handbook and sent home to parents. It should be inviting in its language.

Many schools now list this information on their Web site so that teachers and administrators can be reached by e-mail. Parents should be asked to give e-mail addresses and telephone numbers and indicate when they can be reached.

All of this work is proactive in nature as people are invited to join the change process. How many times have leaders heard someone say, "I didn't know who to call or how to get a hold of them to get the information I needed." This blocking tactic by reluctant followers cannot succeed if a communication system is in place.

## Strategy 13: Establish a Timeline for Goal Implementation

Reluctant followers often fear that they are being asked to change everything they do at once. Some see their jobs as constant change with no time to see whether anything works. Others are fearful that the change process or new goals will eliminate actions that are working for their students. Others give so much time already that they cannot fit one more meeting or idea into their day.

Probably the greatest reluctance among teachers over the past 20 years has been the implementation of technology into the curriculum. Broadening the possibilities for student learning has meant new instructional planning, implementation, and evaluation. With the rapidity of advancements in the use of technology, school leaders have been forced to place other curriculum issues further out on the timeline. Placing technology on the timeline with other goals lets everyone know that all issues are being dealt with and when.

## Strategy 14: When Both Planning and Communicating, Know That Timing Is Everything

When a leader has a choice about when to start the change process, it is essential to offer constituents choices also. Some may want to be more involved at the beginning of the change process, whereas others may need to wait until other school responsibilities are over. A disgruntled high school football coach once said, "I would really like to be a part of these curriculum discussions and decisions, but they hold all of the meetings while I am responsible for 40 students. I have little or no opportunity for input so I get reluctant to follow."

A leader must choose the right time to confront a reluctant follower. Conversations about reluctance must be private, thorough, and not subject to interruption. Hold the calls, shut the door, and listen. If the communication is confrontational in nature, be sure that it is held when you have time to finish the conversation.

Learn to assess the dynamics of your group so that you can judge the responses of participants to timing issues as they emerge. One faculty of reluctant followers, for example, complained that their leader always talked about new changes in the fall but then never started anything until February. By then, all issues had to be explained again, and people thought it was a waste of time. They suggested that goals and actions be offered at the beginning of the year so that they could get started and avoid wasting time later. They also noted that when their leadership asked for input during a meeting, they talked the whole time and had no more than a few minutes at the end of the meeting for teacher and staff input. These teachers saw it as a ploy to keep them from giving input, and they were very mistrustful of the leadership and proposed changes.

## Strategy 15: Provide Accurate Data, Research, and Demographics

Too many reluctant followers have been heard saying, "I have no idea why we are even talking about this. It really does not affect our students or our school." One superintendent, for example, opened a midyear all-district staff meeting by talking about attendance. He asked whether anyone thought there was a problem in the district. Immediately, teachers started talking about problem students and what they could accomplish if the students only came to school. They started brainstorming ways to get parents to send their students to school. The superintendent asked whether they saw any other attendance issues. When they said no, he told them that as the district leader, he was perplexed by an even more serious attendance problem. He then gave a PowerPoint presentation showing that teacher attendance was lower than student attendance. The numbers were there for everyone to see. He then asked what they could do about this problem.

## Strategy 16: Give Accurate Data About Students Regularly

Give positive data first, followed by data that needs to be discussed. Shadow study data; test scores; statistics about school families; the costs of busing, feeding, and cleaning; and consultants' observations can all be used to give staff members information for decision making. Data-driven decision making is essential to move reluctant followers forward. Some principals give little-known but important facts about the district during their morning e-mails and announcements to staff. They are done one at a time so that faculty can informally discuss them, and they help squelch rumors among the staff. Followers who balk at scheduling changes, for example, usually have no idea what numbers the leadership is working with. Even fewer teachers are aware of the laws governing schools and organizations.

## Strategy 17: Accentuate the Positive and Emphasize the Relation of the Data to Current Goals

For example, cite positive statistics in student research: 97% of students have no problem with attendance; 98% of students have not had a discipline referral this month; 74% of students are reading at or above grade level; 81% of students are involved in extracurricular activities. A follow-up memo might add that faculty are welcome to make suggestions for helping the 26% of students who need help in reading. A positive approach to data sends a message to teachers that we are doing a very good job, but we always need to help students who are having problems.

## Strategy 18: Summarize and Debrief

At the end of every meeting, verbally summarize what has been accomplished and then send notes summary to all participants. If you ask a typical student what he or she did in school that day, their answer is usually "Nothing." If you ask a reluctant follower what was decided or discussed in a staff meeting, they will usually give the same response but add the word "important."

The human brain functions better when large doses of information are summarized into three to five major points. Each group meeting or one-on-one conversation with a reluctant follower should end with a summary by the leader. Written summaries for all participants are also helpful in keeping the process moving. For example, one principal who was hoping to improve total school communication asked that minutes of every team meeting be sent by e-mail to the entire staff. When that type of debriefing happened, there was more communication among the staff.

## Strategy 19: Teach People How Groups Work and How to Work in Groups

Understanding the role(s) that they can or do play in the group may ease the reluctance of some followers. Early research classified group behavior into three categories: group task roles, group building and maintenance roles, and individual roles (Benne & Sheats, 1948). These roles are filled by both leaders and followers. The needs and goals of the group dictate the tasks and needed roles. Task roles might include the information seeker, the opinion seeker, the information giver, the opinion giver, the elaborator, the orienter, the critic, the energizer, or the procedural technician.

When groups are functioning effectively, both the task roles and the building and maintenance roles must be considered. Maintenance and building roles focus on the interrelationships among group members. If the group process gets bogged down, the number of reluctant followers will increase. Some informal roles that support the maintenance of relationships and building of group spirit include the encourager, who gives social approval and praise; the mediator, who helps solve member differences; the compromiser, who resolves conflicts between people and ideas; the gatekeeper; the standard setter; the observer; and the follower. The follower passively accepts the ideas of others and is not usually an active member. All of these roles help move the group toward its goals (DeVito, 2006).

## Strategy 20: Assign Group Roles

Although personality affects the comfort level of people in groups, assigned roles can create a positive dynamic as individuals know what is expected of them. Too often, followers are allowed to sit passively through planning meetings and are not required to offer any input. Other groups are dominated by one person seeking leadership, and this creates a new group of reluctant followers.

Group meetings should always include the following assigned task, maintenance, and building roles, which can rotate on a weekly or monthly basis:

- Leader: This person is in charge of organizing the agenda and leading the discussion or tasks to be done.
- Recorder: This person takes minutes of the meeting and distributes them to all parties involved.
- Timer: Some groups appoint a person to keep them on task by limiting the discussion to 10 minutes. A person is appointed to keep track of the time and let them know when the time is up.

- Gatekeeper: This person makes sure that everyone in the group contributes to the discussion if they want to. He or she encourages reluctant members to speak out and makes sure they are not interrupted when they do.

- Technician: This person tapes the meeting or arranges teleconferencing for people in distant places. He or she does the technical work required for the group to function.

These roles can be assigned by the leader or group members can volunteer for them. It is essential, however, that there are identified and assigned roles within the group, that group members know who is doing what, and that group members receive accurate communication.

When all of the proper group roles have been assigned, reluctant followers may show their resistance in a group setting by the individual roles that they display. More reluctant group members may take on the role of the aggressor, blocker, recognition seeker, self-confessor, dominator, help seeker, or special interest pleader (DeVito, 2006). The leader must decide whether to confront these reluctant group members and whether to confront them publicly or privately.

Many school leaders try to let group leadership emerge. Two factors appear to determine how leadership emerges. In groups with undefined leaders, those who participate more tend to emerge as leaders, and those who listen effectively emerge more strongly than those who do not (DeVito, 2006, p. 232).

## Strategy 21: Be Aware of Cultural Differences and Expectations in Group Work

Leaders must be aware of the impact that cultural differences and beliefs have on group work. Some cultures have leaders who lead by birthright and have a long tenure as leader. They are not expected to be democratic as a leader. Others use emergent leadership that is dependent on the task to be done. Some cultures use only male leaders, whereas others are led by the eldest person.

People function in many different groups and thus develop expectations of how groups function. Work groups differ from social groups, which differ from teams. The role of each individual differs according to the function of the group. A person who is a leader in a social group or team situation, for example, may find it difficult to be a follower in a work group. Likewise, work group members who are effective at completing a specific task may lack the skills to function in a social group.

## Strategy 22: Form Listening Triads

One frequently used strategy for involving reluctant followers in a working group is listening triads. This strategy not only involves all group members but also models a strategy that can be used in most classrooms.

This listening activity is useful when an issue requires discussion and may involve conflicting values and beliefs. It can be used by the leader to make sure that all reluctant followers are invited to participate. This activity is timed by the leader to ensure that everyone has an opportunity to speak. There are three roles: the listener, the speaker, and the judge.

To implement listening triads in a group setting, follow this process:

- Step 1: The topic is given by the leader or chosen from the agenda of the group.

- Step 2: Everyone is given two minutes to write down their thoughts about the issue or topic.

- Step 3: The roles are chosen using unbiased criteria—for example, the speaker is the person who lives the farthest from the meeting site; the listener is the person who lives the closest; and the judge lives somewhere in the middle. Everyone has a chance to play all three roles in this activity, so it does not matter who starts.

- Step 4: Announce that notes may not be taken by the listener or the judge; however, the speaker may use notes generated during the two-minute session. The first time this activity is performed, the time limit should be one minute for each speaker, listener, and judge. The amount of time can be increased or decreased depending on the topic or issue.

- Step 5: Encourage people to sit in a triangle so that they can hear each other. Use the following illustration to guide the discussion:

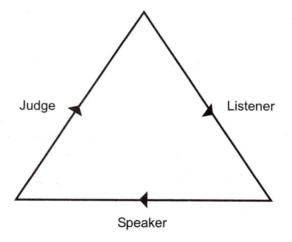

- Step 6: Give the following directions:
  - When the timer says go, the speaker begins to speak to the listener and the judge.
  - At the end of one or two minutes (depending on the agreed-upon time for the issue), the timer gives the stop signal.
  - The listener tells the speaker what he or she said without imparting any judgment about what was said. He or she simply recalls the facts.
  - The listener is given the same amount of time to tell the speaker what he or she said.
  - The judge is then given one minute to decide whether the listener got the facts correct.
  - The leader asks whether there are any questions about the process.
- Step 7: After all of the questions are answered, the leader immediately begins the second round. This time, the speaker is the judge, the listener is speaker, and the judge is the listener. The same process of speaking, listening, and judging continues until everyone has had a chance to speak, listen, and judge.
- Step 8: When everyone is finished, the leader asks that each triad identify three learnings that resulted from the activity. One should be something learned about the process, one should be something learned about the content, and the third should be a general learning. They are given three minutes to generate their learnings (or solutions if a particular problem is being solved). These learnings are then shared with the entire group.
- Step 9: When everyone has shared, the leader may ask individuals to rank their preferences if a solution is being sought. The activity is repeated during several meetings to ensure that everyone is listened to and included in the discussion.

## Strategy 23: Brainstorm for New Ideas or Problem Solving

Group members feel included and are more likely to participate when they are given an opportunity to be a part of brainstorming. It is better for communication if large groups are divided into smaller groups of no more than six. This strategy can be used to generate new ideas, involve all participants, and develop future plans. It can be used when the group is generally reluctant to move forward on an issue. Although some members of the group may offer negative suggestions, they do get a chance to participate. Always give the rules of brainstorming before the group begins:

- Have a timer and recorder.
- Set a five-minute time limit.
- Use the chalkboard, overhead, or newsprint to so that the entire group can see the ideas.
- Any idea is written down without judgment.
- Everyone gets a chance to contribute.
- Small group results are shared with the whole group.
- Whole group results are given to the entire group.

## Strategy 24:
## Use the Literature as the Basis for Discussion

Many leaders have their constituents read a common book in order to motivate or spark discussion among the group and to help with future planning. Businesses and school districts have used both *Good to Great: Why Some Companies Make the Leap—and Others Don't* (2001) and *Built to Last: Successful Habits of Visionary Companies* (1994) by Jim Collins as discussion stimulators. Recently, middle schools have used *This We Believe in Action: Implementing Successful Middle Level Schools* (Erb, 2005) as a way of planning or the future. Whatever the chosen book, the leader should have a clear purpose in mind in asking people to read and respond to it. The book offers a neutral vehicle for communication that does not reflect the bias of any particular person in the building.

## Strategy 25: Model the Type of
## Communication Behavior That You Want

If you want people to talk to you, make yourself available in the hallways, lunchroom, and classrooms. Insist that everyone who greets people be positive and invitational. Train office personnel in how visitors should be greeted. The signs that are posted on school doors can make the people who enter the building feel comfortable or uncomfortable.

Note the subtle difference in two signs that were placed on the doors of schools only four blocks away from each other:

"All visitors must stop in the office for a visitor's pass."

"Welcome to our school. Please stop in the office so we may assist you and give you a visitor's pass."

Though all schools need to post rules for the safety of their students—and some need to restrict visitation because of local violence—all have a choice to communicate that message in a negative or positive way. Negative signs on school doors create reluctance among everyone who enters.

Leaders can create reluctant followers by the language and tone they use in communication. Teachers can create reluctant students in the same way.

## Two Great Communicators

One principal wanted to send home more positive communications about students. During a staff meeting, the staff brainstormed how this could be done and agreed that every team would send at least one positive note home about every student each semester. The principal then showed the staff the large stack of handwritten commendation notes that he had written over the weekend. His own goal was to write a positive note to every student in the school at least once a year.

This policy did more for parental involvement than any other program or activity in the school. When parents heard good news from the school about their child, they began to listen to requests for involvement and participate in classrooms, visioning, and conferences.

Leaders who plan staff development activities and then do not attend the events themselves create reluctant followers. One new superintendent made sure that she attended every staff development activity in her district. Teachers who had been reluctant in the past began to feel that these activities might be important because the superintendent was attending. Both attitude and attendance at staff development improved because she modeled the behavior she expected of others.

## Confronting Reluctant Followers

What happens when you have used all of these strategies and still have one or more reluctant followers? What if Ben There or Don That still refuse to participate or Sam Sarcasm is still sarcastic and rude to others? The leader must decide when and how to confront the reluctant follower.

In his book *Dealing with Difficult Teachers,* Todd Whitaker suggests that the leader should always approach the teacher as if the whole staff were in the room. However, the conversation should be one on one, not one to all (Whitaker, 2002, p. 103). The purpose of a one-on-one conversation is to clear the air and find solutions to problems. Content, timing, and tone of voice are all important. Every conflict that requires a one-on-one conversation relates to values, relationships among colleagues, or the completion of tasks. Many times, difficult conversations are the result of a difference in standards (Sanderson, 2005, 5–6). Whatever the conflict or attempt at resolution, it will require that people meet together and talk. Usually, it is the leader who initiates the conversation. The following strategies may help make a difficult conversation tolerable.

## Strategy 26: One-on-One Conversations

Strategies for dealing with reluctant followers make use of the basic skills of any one-on-one conversation:

- Know your purpose for having the conversation. Clarify your own thoughts and feelings about the issue before the conversation.

- Plan what you are going to cover in the conversation.

- Invite the person you wish to have the conversation with in writing or verbally.

- Find a quiet, private place. Even if you are confronted by a reluctant follower during a meeting, ask that the conversation continue at a time and place where you both can focus on what is being said.

- Make eye contact with the person to whom you are speaking.

- Use sense statements that start with "I." For example, "I sense that you are having difficulty accepting the new faculty curriculum plan for your department," "I sense that you are feeling uncomfortable with the new discipline ideas being expressed by your colleagues," or "I sense that we disagree on the degree of your effectiveness in this planning group."

- Use active listening. Reassure the person that you are listening by paraphrasing what he or she has said. Check for understanding.

- Keep your emotions and temper in check. Try not to show shock or surprise at what is being said. Listen for the real message in what is being said.

- Ask open-ended questions that enable the person to keep talking.

- Summarize what the person has said and ask him or her for alternative ways to solve the problem. If he or she cannot think of any solutions, suggest one or two options that have been tried in similar situations.

- Explore the consequences of each alternative offered. Ask, "If you did that, what might happen?"

- Have the person make a plan of action and tell you what his or her first step will be. Be sure that you can control any action that is taken.

- Arrange for a follow-up conversation to evaluate the person's actions.

Private conversations are better for both people involved, as they take away the audience that the recognition seeker, self-confessor, dominator, or other reluctant followers often seek. Private conversations and confrontations also allow the leader to prepare for the conversation ahead of time. The leader must constantly keep in mind the impact of this individual on the group. Private confrontations and conversations allow the reluctant follower or group disrupter to save face with his or her peers.

Public confrontations among group members or between leaders and group members are rarely pleasant and can cause a real breakdown in the accomplishment of tasks. Leaders must work to depersonalize the comments made, even if they are personal in nature. If a public confrontation by a reluctant follower occurs, the leader must remember to use "I" messages to clarify the issue and keep the conflict from escalating. For example: A group of faculty members had volunteered to explore the possibility of developing a mentoring program for poor readers. At the previous meeting, they had set a goal to find mentors outside the school. This was listed on the agenda as "mentoring program possibilities." As the members were asked to present their findings, a faculty member who had not attended the past meeting and had obviously not read the minutes stood up and said, "I don't believe you think are going to make us add mentoring to our already crowded schedules and class loads. You must know that violates the contract and we are not going to do it. This is just another example of administration cramming something down our throats."

The administrator could easily have reminded the reluctant follower that he had been absent from the last meeting and should have read the minutes. He could have escalated the situation by remarking on class loads compared to other schools or union contracts. Almost any reply could have escalated the conflict and wasted time. Instead, the administrator simply said, "I believe that your concerns will be answered by the committee report, let's hear from them." No escalation, respect for the concerns of the follower, and no waste of time.

## Strategy 27: Use Outside Expertise

Many reluctant followers use old information to make their decisions. They know what they see and believe what they hear from their peers. They may have been using the same lectures and materials for years. When they are asked to use new skills and methods, they balk, close their door, and continue to use the old methods because they lack knowledge or expertise. Outside experts who provide essential information and skill development may get further with theses skeptics because they are outsiders. They are often thought of as apolitical and credible. The old statement that you cannot be a prophet in your own land haunts many leaders when they suddenly find that an idea they have been trying for months or even is completed within weeks once an "expert" says it is alright.

One high school principal, for example, had tried everything in his power to get his staff to look at block scheduling. They refused to even consider the idea and responded with a litany of excuses why it would not work in their school.

Fortunately, they were a respectful group, and so they attended the faculty meeting and listened to a panel of teachers from a nearby high school that had been using block scheduling for three years and loved it. Within a week, several faculty members had approached the principal and asked to see the scheduling options. Hearing those with actual experience gave the needed credibility to the reluctant followers. Though they were still reluctant, they began to seek further information, agreed to visit other schools with block schedules, and tried a pilot program.

### Strategy 28: Use the Classic Dale Carnegie Approach

In the mid-1930s, Dale Carnegie wrote the classic book *How to Win Friends and Influence People.* In his book, he reviewed the successful communication habits of the world's greatest political and business leaders. The book included very commonsense suggestions for dealing with reluctant followers. In his chapter on "Making People Glad to Do What You Want," he cites nine principles for changing attitudes and behavior (Carnegie, 1981, 274–75). These principals were cited indirectly by all of the leaders interviewed for this book. These are not the only suggestions, but those that have worked for leaders over time.

- Begin with praise and honest appreciation.
- Call attention to people's mistakes indirectly.
- Talk about your own mistakes before criticizing the other person.
- Ask questions instead of giving direct orders.
- Let the other person save face.
- Praise the slightest improvement and praise every improvement.
- Give the other person a fine reputation to live up to.
- Use encouragement. Make the fault seem easy to correct.
- Make the other person happy about doing the thing you suggest.

### Strategy 29: Celebrate Small Successes Along the Way

Recognition can come in the form of written praise, verbal recognition at a meeting, or special scheduling perks. One leader who had been having difficulty getting teachers to volunteer for the planning committee used his budget to hire substitutes so that those who volunteered could meet for a full teaching day at an off-site location.

When teachers saw an opportunity to have a meeting at which they could really get something substantial done, those who had been reluctant volunteered. They saw the time as a reward for their efforts. In the undisturbed location, they accomplished more in one day than they had accomplished in several after-school meetings during the year. Success is often celebrated with food, and every person interviewed for this book said that he or she had learned early on that staff members lose some of their reluctance when recognition includes a cup of coffee and a donut.

## Strategy 30: Communicate the Reality of the Situation to Those Who Will Not Change

When there is a true conflict of values and practices within an organization, those who are not willing to accept change must be reevaluated for their current level of functioning and the impact of their attitude on other members of the group. One superintendent said that he used the following statement to deal with those who would not change and were not doing an effective job. "This school district is like a moving bus. It is moving forward. It is not parked and it is certainly not in reverse. We expect that everyone will be one the bus, but if you are not happy here, I will certainly support your efforts to find happiness on a different bus."

Another said he usually called in the reluctant person and said, "I know that you are reluctant to change and adopt this program. Please tell me how I can help you so that we can keep your current position."

Most offered both short- and long-term plans of action for the employee and documented every action that was or was not made. Most documentation came from direct observation. Documentation, not hearsay, is essential to helping a person change.

### Documentation

One principal in a school in which teachers were having problems with classroom management asked that video cameras be placed in several classrooms each day on a random basis. The assumption was that student behavior would improve if they were being recorded. What the principal found was that teaching methods were much more dynamic and students more involved when the classrooms were being recorded. The principal used data from the tapes to recognize good teaching and good behavior.

### Evaluation of the Group's Progress

The final element in developing a communication strategy to work with reluctant followers is to evaluate the progress of the group. This ongoing evaluation can be as simple as committee reports at faculty meetings or as complex as faculty, parent, and student surveys. Many times, the leader will ask the constituents what type of evaluation they would find most useful and implement their ideas.

Many leaders use a summary strategy at the end of each meeting to ensure that everyone understands what was or was not decided. Summaries are then written and shared with all necessary and involved personnel.

If the leader finds that there is a significant number of reluctant followers who are not making progress toward the goals of the organization, then it is time to begin having one-on-one conversations.

Success stories from leaders who affected significant change within a system that had many reluctant followers are full of examples of communication strategies. One such story illustrates the strategies that have been listed in this chapter.

## A Communication Success Story

West Middle School was a traditional miniature junior high school. The principal was given the charge from the assistant superintendent to implement the middle school concept. Later in his career, the same leader transformed another school into a participating school in the Essential Schools program. The communication strategies and processes he used with reluctant staff members were very similar.

There were many uninformed reluctant followers who felt that they were already doing a good job. The principal knew that he would have to build his own knowledge base and a support base within his staff. During the transition to middle school, he first bought books for everyone to read about the middle school. He used his budget to send staff members to state and local conferences and on school visitations to excellent middle schools.

Second, he identified staff members who were most dependable and put them in charge of study groups. He put one reluctant teacher in each of the groups. The goal of the groups was to study the concept and see what they could implement within their school. The directive from the leader was that all decisions were to be based on what was best for the students. He wanted all groups to have a sound basis for their decision making, and he relied on knowledge and peer pressure to bring along the reluctant followers.

He then invited staff members to write grants that would enhance their teaching and transition. Grants would also allow implementation of the schoolwide goals that had been written as a staff.

In one-on-one conferences, he consistently praised those who changed and rewarded them by sending them to conferences, making presentations to the board of education, and giving them excellent yearly evaluations. Their acceptance of change was recognized and communicated to them.

He led as a risk taker who was willing to step outside the box and implement new practices. Though support from the central office was essential, none of the changes would have occurred without this leader's willingness to take the necessary risks and model that behavior for his faculty.

During this process, he observed several characteristics of reluctant staff members:

- They avoided all new methods and materials.
- They spoke out openly in the teacher's work room against the changes.
- They ignored the changes or simply made excuses for why they could not change.
- Some bid out entirely and asked for transfers within the district, whereas others sought community support for their refusal to change by talking in beauty salons, barbershops, churches, and local community meetings.
- Some filed grievances, and others retired early.

There were all levels of reluctance within one faculty.

The strategies this leader used to deal with this reluctance included the following:

- Putting all of the teachers in teams and study groups so that information was coming from peers rather than the leader.
- Meeting at an off-site location where everyone could be comfortable and focused.
- Counseling reluctant staff members one on one in a professional manner. Typically, the conversation focused on one thing: "We need to see changes in your classroom, so what can we do to help you make those changes?"
- Organizing a peer coaching program in which teachers visited other classes and discussed what they saw after each visit.
- Adding changes to teachers' goals for the next year and showing them how they could accomplish those goals (this was done in yearly evaluation conferences).
- Preaching against negativism and inviting gripers and complainers to go someplace else. This leader's watchword was, "We have a right to be happy, positive, and carry on our work." Nip griping and complaining in the bud.
- Involving parents and community leaders in the change process. Encourage them to be visible and visit classrooms. Parent visits

kept teachers on their toes. The association of parents and teachers met monthly and selected people to work on the leadership team.

- ◆ Bringing in outside resources for the continued learning of all staff members.
- ◆ Putting the teachers on buses and having them ride the routes to see where their students were coming from.
- ◆ Having pep rallies for academics to communicate the goals of academic achievement to the students.
- ◆ Encouraging reluctant staff members to leave the building if they could not accept the changes.

This leader was successful with most reluctant staff members because he lead by example, outworked the hardest-working staff member, was always positive and professional, listened well, and learned to correctly interpret what others were saying.

All of the changes implemented at West Middle School were the result of faculty decision making, with the leader's guidance. When all of the changes had been determined, a decision-making team was established that included every team leader, a student from each grade, three parents, and one community leader. They met Thursdays from 7:00 to 8:00 a.m. and made decisions for the school. The principal agreed to implement their ideas as long as they did not violate board policy or get the principal fired. The team leader reports kept all teachers informed. This school became an often-visited demonstration school for many other middle schools in the state of Illinois.

When asked what advice this leader would give to new leaders facing systemic change in their buildings, he said, "Take pride in small steps. Praise repeatedly. Keep your emotions under control. Love your job as a change agent and work with a passion. Be sure that everyone in school is there for the kids and always direct everything toward their good." Wise words from a leader who went on the become Illinois Principal of the Year, an National Association of Secondary School Principals/Burger King Principal of the Year, a Thomson Fellow at Brown University, president of the Illinois Principals Association, a member of the Illinois Curriculum Council, president of the Association of Illinois Middle Schools, and the founder of the Alton Excellence Award.

The Alton Excellence Award is given to two students from each school every year. There is an awards dinner and recognition for the students. Principals wash cars and have other fund-raisers to pay for the dinner. This award is still in existence. When this leader retired, the middle school was merged with another school that had never really made the transition. Most staff members continued to implement what they had learned from their original middle school and Essential Schools transitions. They continue to be active in state and local associations. As this leader once said, "During my first year as a principal I ran my building. In the second year, I worked with my staff and that has made all the difference in the world." (Interview with Mr. Tom Gunning, 2006.)[1]

## Summary

There are four essential processes for diminishing the number of people who say, "Lead me—I dare you." Motivation, inclusion, communication, and evaluation form the outline of practical strategies that can help leaders involve all group members in planning, implementing, and evaluating change. The skill of listening to others, plus having a communication plan, made a difference in every school. Knowing how groups work, how to have supportive one-on-one conversations, and how to get people to work together were also cited as essential skills.

## Resources

Benne, K. D., & Sheats, P. (1948). Functional roles of group members. *Journal of Social Issues, 4,* 41–49.

Carnegie, D. (1981). *How to win friends and influence people* (Rev. ed.). New York: Simon & Schuster.

Collins, J. C. (2001). *Good to great: Why some companies make the leap—and others don't.* New York: HarperBusiness.

Collins, J. C., & Porras, J. I. (1994). *Built to last: Successful habits of visionary companies.* New York: HarperBusiness.

DeVito, J. A. (2006). *Human communication: The basic course* (10th ed.). Boston: Allyn and Bacon

Erb, T. O. (Ed.). (2005). *This we believe in action: Implementing successful middle level schools.* Westerville, OH: National Middle School Association.

Fullan, M., Bertani, A., & Quinn, J. (2004). New lessons for districtwide reform. *Educational Leadership, 61*(7), 42.

Gunning, T. (2006, July). Interview with the author.

Lounsbury, J. H., & Clark, D. C. (1990). *Inside grade eight: From apathy to excitement.* Reston, VA: National Association of Secondary School Principals.

Lounsbury, J. H., & Johnston, J. H. (1985). *How fares the ninth grade?* Reston, VA: National Association of Secondary School Principals.

Lounsbury, J. H., & Johnston, J. H. (1988). *Life in the three sixth grades.* Reston, VA.; National Association of Secondary School Principals.

Lounsbury, J., Marani, J., & Compton, M. (1980). *The middle school in profile: A day in the seventh grade.* Columbus, OH: National Middle School Association.

Sanderson, B. E. (2005). *Talk it out! The educator's guide to successful difficult conversations.* Larchmont, NY: Eye On Education.

Whitaker, T. (2002). *Dealing with difficult teachers* (2nd ed.). Larchmont, NY: Eye On Education.

[1]Tom Gunning is retired from the Alton, Illinois public schools and state committees.

# 7

# Helping Followers Become Leaders

One school needed new computers for their students and staff. But the school's limited budget and state cutbacks made the dream seem impossible, until the superintendent listened to two parents with a funding idea. They volunteered to plan and implement a major fund-raiser for the school.

Using the skills they learned in the business world, they organized a dinner dance with an auction. What was different about this auction was that all of the items were made by the children in the school.

The parents involved each classroom, every teacher, all of the students, and most of the parents. Teachers got very excited about the products being made in their classrooms. The kindergarten children put their handprints on three large pieces of white plastic that were wrapped around PVC pipe to become teepees. They should have made 10, as they sold for $600 each at the auction. The eighth grade took the money that the students had earned at a car wash and bought dog supplies. They made up fancy baskets for dog owners that sold for more than $100 each. The superintendent was amazed when the parents presented him with a check for $18,000 from the dinner dance and auction. Given the opportunity to lead, parents can work small miracles in a school district.

As a leader, he knew the value of using the talents of those who had been following.

Changing schools require multiple leaders. If the process is truly inclusive, there will be teacher leaders, student leaders, parent leaders, and community leaders who plan, implement, and evaluate different phases of this ongoing process.

# Developing Parent Involvement and Leadership

Developing parent involvement and leadership leads to closer communication and stronger teacher–parent–student bonds. Many leaders want to change the way that middle and high school parents look at school. For many parents, their involvement ends when their child leaves elementary school and enters the world of many teachers, changing classes, multiple expectations, and puberty. Parents are often concerned about how they can help out at the middle or high school when their students do not want them there.

When the Waukegan, Illinois middle schools wanted to celebrate the diversity of their population, it was a parent team that planned and implemented all of the activities for an entire year. When another middle school wanted to expand the activities offered during its Friday afternoon elective program, it sent a letter to all parents asking for help and talent. They received more than 175 responses, offers of help, and topics that parents could teach students. Topics ranged from Cajun cooking to basic Japanese. Though the mini-courses were only one hour, the program gave parents confidence that they could be a part of the school and do something productive. What followed was the development—by the parents—of a yearly arts festival that relied on volunteers from the community who were professionals in the arts. That program would not have been possible without parent leadership. In addition to fund-raising and program development, parents can also serve as mentors, tutors, and even teachers.

High school leaders who recognize the value of parent leadership may give parents the task of organizing career days, trips for clubs, and special events for students. Most school vision committees include parents throughout the process. Parent leadership can be developed when the administrator encourages and allows parents to make their talents available to teachers. For example, middle and high school parents in one district created systemic change in the way conferences took place when they objected to long lines, impersonal reports, and the scheduling of conferences during the workday.

In one school, teachers had held conferences in the same way for 30 years because it was tradition. Parents who were on principal's advisory council asked that conferences be the top priority of the year. As the council investigated what other successful schools in the area were doing, they determined that they needed to implement student-led conferences. It was not an easy task to convince the teachers, but the parents presented convincing arguments about the value to the students.

During the Month of the Young Adolescent, sponsored by the National Middle School Association, parents are invited to spend an entire day with their child at school. They go to classes, eat lunch, and participate with their son or daughter. From those experiences, parents have become more willing to volunteer in the schools.

Some schools have gym space available at night and ask parents at each grade level to plan a family night there. Three-on-three basketball is popular, but so are parent–student Olympics and line dancing. Once the school leader encourages parents, they will take the lead and design important events for students. Many high schools offer classes for parents who wish to finish their own high school education. This connection to the school increases their leadership and involvement.

## Call Me—I Dare You!
## Involving Reluctant Parents

Reluctant parents lack not only leadership but also total involvement with their child and the school. A worthy goal for teachers and leaders is to make them a part of the school in some positive way. Parents are always invited to participate in transitions from elementary to middle and middle to high school. Parents who cannot physically attend can be sent messages by phone, e-mail, or other types of print and visual media.

Research by Seidman, Lambert, Allen, and Aber (2003) found that both attendance and parent involvement improve when families are involved in the process. But there are still those phantom parents who are never seen by the school. Good questions for school leaders to ask children are, "When is a good time to reach your parent or guardian?" and "Where is the best place to reach them?" Too often, the numbers given on enrollment cards are not accurate, and families don't know how to change them.

Reluctant parents may be coerced by their children to come to school if the children are offered a small reward. One very clever team of teachers wanted to have all parents attend a team presentation on the outdoor education program they were planning. They told the students that if their parents attended, they would get a free brownie at lunch the next day. As parents whom the team had not seen before signed in, the teachers marveled once again at the importance of food to young adolescents. The teachers took the opportunity to say something nice about each student whose parents were in attendance. When parents do not feel threatened by the school environment, they are more likely to go. Sometimes the key to involving reluctant parents is to get their children to remind them.

Parents can be involved as volunteers and community collaborators. What is essential is that communication go both ways between the parents and the school. Leaders must help parents understand whom they can call with their concerns and questions. "One challenge is to ensure that there are parent representatives on school committees from all of the racial and ethnic, socioeconomic groups, and geographic communities present in the schools" (Epstein, 2005, p. 84).

As the school leader, when talking to parents, always ask for their help or their thoughts in addressing school concerns. Communities are full of parents who can and will assert themselves and help the school.

## Developing Students as Leaders

Developing student leaders and leadership skills are goals of most schools. The strategies for developing student leadership may depend on the age of the students, the location of the school, and the types of mentors who are available. Even students who are at risk of academic failure have been found to take leadership roles when they are given a challenge that suits their particular talents. Student government leaders, for example, can have a major impact on community voters when they research and present issues. Athletes can serve as informal leaders in the school and community because of their commitment to practice and teamwork.

Developing student leadership means giving students opportunities to learn, practice, and develop the skills of leadership. Leadership skills are observable in students as early as elementary school when they organize playground activities, take on the school bully, or ask a teacher whether they can involve the school in a community project. In middle schools, leadership skills emerge in athletics, student government, community service projects, team projects, science fairs, and in response to needs and injustices in the world. Principals who recognize the need to provide leadership opportunities for students will often invite students to be a part of the school planning committee.

## Leadership Training Clubs for Students

Organizations such as the Builders Clubs and Key Clubs sponsored by Kiwanis International and Future Business Leaders of America provide national programs that give students a chance to practice leadership at the local level. One school's Builders Club invited a garden club to join them in creating a butterfly garden in an unused and ugly section of their school yard. The adults in the garden club were amazed at the leadership skills of the students. The result was a garden that is used by photographers, science classes, artists, school classes, and writers. The students and garden club members continue to keep the garden blooming every year.

Another school's Future Business Leaders Club designed and operated a mall in the hallway during the holiday season. Each student in the club led a group of interested students in the design and manufacturing of a product that could be sold in the mall. Jewelry, food, and crafts were popular items. The faculty leader merely facilitated the process for these enthusiastic students.

In 1996, the Future Business Leaders Club developed a curriculum for leadership skill development. They identified the following leadership building blocks for students:

- Developing a vision
- Building self-awareness
- Collecting and using information
- Making decisions
- Communicating

In this training module, the students are asked to develop their own definition of what makes a leader. They are asked to do the following:

- Identify and develop a rationale explaining the importance of relationships as a basis for initiating leadership and teamwork skills and behaviors
- Identify leadership characteristics and teamwork skills and behaviors that they have observed
- Identify which of those skills and behaviors they have initiated
- List ways in which they can refine their skills
- Develop a class report on their experiences. (FBLA, p. 87)

Among the essential elements of learning to be a leader are the development of relationships, conflict resolution, service, and looking for possibilities in the school and community.

When one compares those skills to the ones listed in most leadership books for businesses and schools, they are the same. The main difference is that adolescents do not have the same frame of reference and experience that adults have. Providing leadership training and involvement in decision making is one of the key components in helping all students, particularly at-risk students, survive and thrive (Brough, Bergmann, & Holt, 2006). Community service allows students to learn leadership skills from leaders outside the school.

Vocational programs allow students to develop and demonstrate talents in ways that may not be possible in a traditional school curriculum. Large vocational organizations such as Delta Epsilon Chi and Skills USA give students leadership training in their chosen field and provide competitions and opportunities to excel in their chosen vocation. Watching a team of young chefs prepare a five-course gourmet meal in 30 minutes, for example, is a lesson in leadership and teamwork in action.

When school leaders offer program such as the Builders Club, the Future Business Leaders Club, Junior Achievement, and decision-making classes, they are welcoming the development of leadership in their students. When students elect their own student government and those students have a say in what happens in the school, leadership develops. For example, a group of high school students was instrumental in changing the menu in their high school cafeteria as they surveyed students, developed an alternate plan, and presented it to the school board for approval. Their leadership created more choice and healthier selections for everyone.

Although summer leadership camps are available for middle and high school students, schools can offer similar leadership training for students during the school year. An increasing number of high schools require community service in order to graduate. Designing and planning a service project requires students to use leadership and communication skills. Many high schools now require portfolios that students keep throughout high school and present during an interview in their senior year.

This portfolio includes their goals, accomplishments, and samples of their best work. They are responsible for the contents of the portfolio and must take the initiative to complete it, present it, and evaluate the process. Students learn to recognize their own leadership skills during the portfolio development process. They can ask for help if they feel they need a mentor for a particular skill.

In addition to portfolios and interviews, many school offer decision-making classes, seminars, and career shadowing programs. Athletes get weekly opportunities to practice their leadership skills on the field, court, or other place of competition. Students who excel academically can earn an invitation to special academic events such as the Junior Senator program, where they can practice their own leadership skills while observing how government works.

Reluctant students, like reluctant teachers, need the same four elements from their leadership: motivation, inclusion, communication, and evaluation. When students feel they are a part of their own school process, they are more apt to practice leadership. Schools provide a wealth of opportunities for students to get involved in after-school programs in the arts, athletics, and content-area clubs. Some students are involved in everything, some in nothing. School leaders should be sure that someone invites those reluctant students to participate and follows through on their involvement.

One school asked all students to list every organized activity they were involved in, both in and outside school. Some students were involved in a religious activity outside school, and many others had jobs. If a student was not involved in any activity, a team of teachers, administrators, and counselors would have a conference with that student to find out what he or she would like to be involved in. What they found was that there was a fairly large group of students who liked to sit home and read. When asked whether they would like to talk with other students about books just for fun, they all said they probably would. So the school gave them a place to meet, asked them to choose a common book, and called the group Oprah's Other Book Club. Those reluctant participants were included in something in the school that was of interest to them.

## Professional Learning Communities and Distributive Leadership

Given the myriad tasks, complications, and paperwork now required of school administrators, it only makes sense to build teacher leadership in the school. The diversity of school challenges leads us to believe that one person cannot solve all of the problems in isolation. Individuals and groups need to step up to the plate to assume some leadership—once thought to be the realm of the principal. Teachers are, after all, the frontline troops when dealing with students and, often, with parents.

Harris (2003) describes a professional learning community as an organization in which teachers and their leaders share a sense of purpose, collaborate in decision making, and accept joint responsibility for the outcomes of their decisions. Eaker, DuFour, and Burnette (2002) make the case that professional learning communities should focus on student learning rather than teachers or teaching. The beauty of this organizational structure is that teachers are less threatened as they become more student centered. It is not about them—it's about the students.

Dr. Bess Scott articulates this mission daily in her e-mail messages to her faculty, asking, "How are we articulating our learning expectations to our students?" She invites and even expects dialogue about how to ensure that students are achieving at grade level or above (see the success story at the end of Chapter 5). This includes a clear response to students who are exhibiting difficulties. Overcoming such difficulties becomes a community challenge rather than a task that is left to one teacher's devices. In this way, teachers and administrators support one another in their shared mission, which decreases reluctant followers' complaints.

The implementation of a professional learning community structure includes a reorientation of teacher and administrator attitudes. Because it tends to be proactive rather than reactive, a professional learning community approach can take advantage of teachers' talents and skills in a positive light while collaborating to meet daily challenges. By definition, a professional learning community requires conversations among stakeholders as they strive to enculturate their shared values. It is a positive, collaborative, and optimistic approach to meeting the challenges presented in an active learning community. In a Professional Learning Community, "administrators are viewed as leaders of leaders [while] teachers are viewed as transformational leaders" (Eaker, 2002, p. 22).

Similarly, proponents of distributive leadership argue that the hierarchical nature of many schools is not as effective as a structure that spreads leadership tasks among stakeholders (see, e.g., http://www.e3smallschools.org/dl.html). Distributive leadership, like the Professional Learning Community, encourages teachers to take ownership of student success. Rather than the principal delegating authority, it is the stakeholders who work collaboratively to assume responsibility for specific tasks of the academic program. Logically, teachers assume ownership of the instructional program, and parents work to engage the community in support of school efforts. Also known as "collective leadership," this approach distributes decision making and thus feelings of ownership among all the stakeholders of the school, including the students. It's difficult to remain reluctant when you are partially responsible and in charge.

In his doctoral dissertation, Alan Moyer (2006) concludes that teachers need to be better prepared to become leaders. He found that certain areas of communications, self-management, and leadership were rated lower than skills such as planning and controlling or meeting commitments. Clearly, staff development for teachers could focus on leadership building and communication skills, including how to collaborate effectively for the overall welfare of the students. Teacher difficulties that are the result of communication problems are much less likely to occur in such a collaborative and collegial organization.

## Staff Development for Leadership

How wonderful it would be to have a school full of teacher leaders who collaborate for the achievement of all children in their care. Part of the task for achieving that dream is to help teachers reach their own potential. So often, staff development focuses on a component of teaching (e.g., making rubrics) rather than the development of self as a leader and wise decision maker. Teachers and administrators need to be readers of the educational literature, a luxury to most of us in the field. But how can educators be true professionals if they can't keep up with the professional dialogue? Effective administrators realize that good ideas arise from good dialogue, which arises from reading good literature. So they make time for reading and sharing. Many schools now purchase the same book or provide the same article for the entire staff, then have "book talks" about what they have learned (see Chapter 6 for some titles). Some teams of teachers designate a planning period each month for the discussion of an important issue they have researched. People have a difficult time regarding themselves as leaders if they're being talked at all the time.

Another good use of staff development time is the determination of personality type (described in Chapter 3). Teachers can then use that information not only to learn how to become better collaborators but also to reach the needs of their diverse student body. This kind of staff development fosters collegiality and discussions of human development and characteristics. It encourages people to get to know each other rather than rely on often-faulty perceptions.

Finally, staff development ought to help teachers become better leaders by encouraging them to give constructive feedback to students and peers, to learn how to deal with and resolve conflict, to set meaningful goals, and to evaluate themselves—all skills that good teachers should model for their students (see the activity in Chapter 8). Reflective practitioners look inward to determine how they can better address a challenge rather than merely complain about it. They think in a structured way about their attitudes and behaviors. Figure 7.1 delineates some of the levels of reflection.

## Attributes of Self-Reflection

| High Self-Reflection | Medium Self-Reflection | Low Self-Reflection |
| --- | --- | --- |
| • Focuses on details and gives specific examples | • Identifies ideas but does not provide a full discussion | • Holds vague ideas |
| • Covers many points | • Begins to take ownership | • Makes simple restatements |
| • Engages in self-revelation | • Describes performance but leaves out rationale | • Gives only descriptions |
| • Evidences motivation | • Focuses on only a few ideas | • Focuses mainly on surface features |
| • Sets goals for the future | • Considers content, context, or process but not all three | • Reports obvious content with no new insights |
| • Considers content, context, and process | • Is sometimes inaccurate with theory applications | • Gives no examples |
| • Takes thinking risks | • Doesn't seem completely honest | • Says "I like it"/"I don't like it" |

| High Self-Reflection | Medium Self-Reflection | Low Self-Reflection |
|---|---|---|
| • Supports growth with examples | • Lacks sincerity | • Is one-dimensional |
| • Is organized | • Describes key events that affect thinking but does not compare over time | • Is superficial |
| • Is sincere and honest | • Requires inferences about what is meant | • Has low to no awareness of the need to set goals or make progress |
| • Gives comparisons of personal thinking over time | • Does not explain connections completely | • Is inaccurate |
| • Shares feelings but includes theory anchors | • Own learning is not well articulated | • Has no personal ownership of ideas |
| • Examines both strengths and weaknesses | | • Is disorganized—difficult to follow meaning |
| • Does in-depth analysis | | • Beliefs are based only on own experience; doesn't value other perspectives |
| • Provides good reasons and explanations | | • Doesn't accept evidence |
| • Reveals thoughts | | |
| • Develops a personal voice and ownership of ideas | | |
| • Examines skill improvements | | |
| • Gives personal reaction | | |
| • Sets goals and looks ahead | | |
| • Considers ethics | | |
| • Views experiences from many perspectives | | |

*Source:* Chart adapted from Arter, J., & McTighe, J. *Scoring rubrics in the classroom*, pp.39–40, copyright 2001, Thousand Oaks, CA: Corwin Press, Inc. Reprinted by permission of Corwin Press, Inc.

Staff development in a school community should embody the philosophy of the school. It should focus on learning, self-improvement, collaboration, and trust.

## Success Story: Helping Followers Become Leaders

This principal exudes optimism and high expectations. He and his teacher colleagues collaborate to continually make improvements to their professional learning community. All teachers are expected to take their turns in teacher leadership positions, and they are held accountable for their work. He says that he focuses on a teacher's behaviors rather than his or her attitudes: "Attitudes will come around when staff members are convinced this collaborative time is valuable and will impact student achievement and guide their instruction in the classroom."

He gives constructive criticism freely but in a way that is nonthreatening. He asks teachers to reflect on their response or work and asks, "How else might you have done it?" He demonstrates his belief that teachers want to be effective, so he freely gives his time and energies to provide feedback and help teachers see different ways of approaching a problem. He believes that building strong professional relationships is the key to an effective school culture. An effective principal lives his philosophy by working hard, having high expectations for his students and staff, helping the school community set and make progress toward meaningful goals, and telling the truth. (Interview with Al Moyer, 2006.)[1]

## Success Story: Involving Everyone and Leading Change in a Negative Environment

The teachers, parents, and community were not sure they could trust the administration when the board of education decided for a second time to change the junior high schools to middle schools. The idea for the changes was generated and investigated during the district strategic planning process. Teachers had been ready for the change a few years before, but then there were cutbacks and union issues. Established staff members felt cheated and lost faith in the system. When the board decided to try the middle school concept again, administrators had to first restore faith in the system.

The task of making the changes and restoring faith in the system was given to a middle school principal who had made significant changes in his own building in spite of the district climate. He was appointed as assistant superintendent of instruction and given several changes to make at all levels of the district schools. His own first superintendent had told him that "rapid change comes slowly," and he soon came to understand what that meant. He encountered every type of resister identified in this book. He had people from every level of resistance, including some who were in building leadership positions. Parents were not sure what to think of the proposed changes and had to be included in the planning and implementation.

Most people are resistant to change in some way. They think change is good for others but not for themselves. Many of the people whom this leader faced feared change and had a sense of resentment stemming from their belief that they had done something wrong. Many reluctant followers took the attempts at change personally, immediately assuming that they were in the wrong.

There were issues of power and control. On the staff, there were people who were trying to be in control and resisted because of the power struggle. Parents wanted facts, and they demanded to know how this change would affect their children. Board members wanted numbers that would assure parents that this change would raise test scores. There were other reluctant followers, too:

- People who were adamantly opposed the change and vocalized their opposition at meetings
- Passive-aggressive people who didn't say anything but closed their classroom doors and refused to change
- Fence-sitters who went along with the majority
- People who were willing to change but were not motivated to do sp on their own—they needed to be pushed and encouraged
- Trailblazers who were always willing to do new things in the classroom—they focused on the best interest of the students

The administrators focused on the trailblazers and did an assessment of the staff to find out who was at each level. They could not make assumptions but had to get a sense of who the players were by talking to teachers, students, and parents. There was no correlation between vocal opposition and poor teaching, and vocal opponents had to be listened to.

The strategies that were used to move this district forward helped bring those vocal opponents into the majority. Some of the strategies used included the following:

- Talk to everyone, listen to everyone, and then talk some more.
- Find out who the risk takers are. Support their efforts. In this district, one of the best teachers refused to talk at faculty meetings because she had been put down so vehemently in the past.
- Give everyone a clear reason why the change is going to make a difference.
- Show everyone how the change will benefit students.
- Listen to teachers' ideas...they have a good sense of what needs to be done.
- Recognize the positive things that people are doing when they take a risk.
- Shift the focus from teachers to students by gathering student data.
- Slowly shift the culture away from engrained habits.
- Carefully select small working groups and place only one naysayer in each group...and hope you don't have to place one in each group.
- Realize there will be opposition and criticism. Leaders who were well accepted as teachers may be severely criticized when they become administrators.
- Bring in long-term consultants for systemic change. Have them collect and present data to staff.
- Build on staff ideas...accept their ideas and give them ownership. In this district, the exploratory teachers wanted to be a team. Because the suggestion had come from them, they worked diligently to make it work in spite of horrendous scheduling problems.
- Implement a strategic planning and visioning process. Publish the timeline.
- Bring school board members, parents, and students along with the planning by inviting them to in-service meetings, giving them reading materials, putting them on study groups, and letting them communicate with the community.
- Set up a communication system to give regular progress reports.
- Ask principals, parents, and staff members to attend conferences and workshops together and then report back to the entire group.
- Get people excited about the possibilities. Get all the dreams down on the strategic plan and then look at the curriculum and finances. As part of the initial plan in this district, all ideas were ac-

cepted as possible. There was no discussion of why an idea would not work. All ideas were investigated.

- Build consensus by reaching out to individuals who are fence-sitters. Help them understand their role in the change process.

These strategies, in addition to the positive, consistent, and compassionate leadership of the assistant superintendent, allowed the district to make extensive changes, and implement exemplary programs with a new climate of trust and cooperation. The leader had no problem moving people around in the district if the change met his criteria: It had to benefit the students.

When the leader of this transition was asked about the characteristics of a good leader, he listed the following:

- Children have to be the focus. Too often, finances or teacher interests overcome that focus, and it is up to the leader to maintain the focus.
- Listen.
- Practice effective communication with clear goals and a focus on the children.
- Be knowledgeable about current issues and topics. Read, read, read.
- Be persistent but not dogmatic.
- Be willing to accept criticism.
- Be able to dust yourself off and get back to work after making a mistake.
- Know that leaders will always have resisters—not all people will buy in to what you are doing.
- Recognize that no matter what level you are leading, resistance does not change.

When asked what advice he would give a new principal, this leader said,

- Be empathetic with people.
- Recognize efforts, even small ones.
- Know that people respect leaders who are not in it for themselves but for the kids.
- Take your job seriously, but don't take yourself seriously.
- Maintain a sense of humor.
- Find the people the resources they need to do their job.
- Don't assume anything.

Bill Burke is one of many leaders who, on a daily basis, offer the kind of leadership it takes to make systemic change in a school district. He recently

retired from his leadership position and coaches school improvement plans in McHenry County, Illinois.
(Interview with William Burke, 2006.)[2]

## Resources

Arter, J., & McTighe, J. (2001). *Scoring rubrics in the classroom: Using performance criteria for assessing and improving student performance.* Thousand Oaks, CA: Corwin Press.

Brough, J. A., Bergmann, S., & Holt, L. C. (2006). *Teach me—I dare you!* Larchmont, NY: Eye On Education.

Burke, W. (2006, August). Interview with the author, McHenry, IL.

Eaker, R. (2002). Cultural shifts: Transforming schools into professional learning communities. In R. Eaker, R. DuFour, & R. Burnette (Eds.), *Getting started: Restructuring schools to become professional learning communities* (pp. 9–29). Bloomington, IN: National Educational Service.

Eaker, R., DuFour, R., & Burnette, R. (2002). *Getting started: Restructuring schools to become professional learning communities.* Bloomington, IN: National Educational Service.

Epstein, J. (2005). School-initiated family and community partnerships, in ThisWe Believe in action: Implementing successful middle schoools. Westerville, OH: National Middle School Association.

Erb, T. O. (Ed.). (2005). This we believe in action: Implementing successful middle level schools. Westerville, OH: National Middle School Association.

Fullan, M. (2001). *Leading in a culture of change.* San Francisco: Jossey-Bass.

Harris, A. (2003). Teacher leadership as distributed leadership: Heresy, fantasy, or possibility? School Leadership and Management, 23, 313–324.

Moyer, A. (2006). *Gauging the existing leadership effectiveness of middle school teacher team leaders for the formation of a professional learning community.* Unpublished doctoral dissertation, Immaculata University.

Seidman, E., Lambert, L., Allen, L., & Aber, J. L. (2003). Urban adolescents' transition to junior high school and protective family transactions. *Journal of Early Adolescence, 23,* 166–193.

### Organizations

Builders Club of America, Kiwanis International. www.buildersclub.org. The largest community service club for middle schools in the world.

Delta Epsilon Chi. www.deca.org. The marketing and business leadership training club for high school and college students.

Future Business Leaders of America, Phi Beta Lambda. www.fbla.org

Junior Achievement. www.ja.org. Clubs provide training in business leadership for middle and high school students.

Key Clubs of America. www.keyclub.org. High school service clubs sponsored by Kiwanis International (high school version of the Builders Clubs).

National Association of Elementary School Principals. www.NAESP.org

National Middle School Association. www.nmsa.org.

National Association of Secondary School Principals. www.nassp.org.

SkillsUSA. www.skillsusa.org. The vocational industrial club of America; provides leadership and skills training for vocational students.


[1]Mr. Al Moyer is currently the principal at E.H. Marker Intermediate School in Southwestern School District, Hanover, PA.

[2]Mr. William Burke is retired from the McHenry, Illinois Public Schools and currently coaching school improvement plans for local schools.

# 8

# Confronting Those Who Will Not Change: Who Killed Learning in the Seventh Grade?

This chapter presents a staff development exercise that facilitates planning and discussion about good teaching. This exercise is a mystery in several parts that can be used during a faculty meeting or staff development day. It is intended to be a catalyst for discussion about good teaching and the change process. The names are fictitious and have been written as composites with no one teacher in mind. The goal is to foster an awareness of the ways that attitude, style, and practice affect students and the change process in schools.

Although a middle school is given in this example, the age level of the students and the nurse's report can be changed to illustrate any grade level you choose. Leaders who have used this simulation in the past always send in one more name to be added. Leaders should preface this activity with a purpose statement and a brief discussion of how we all, as humans, do some of the things in the exercise…however, the real issue is that some teachers have made these a permanent teaching style. This exercise can be used at a single meeting if there is enough time for the discussion and activities that are part of Phases II and III. Make sure there is time for the generation of positive attitudes and plenty of discussion.

Be sure to copy and separate the characters before the meeting so that they can be distributed at random. Do not simply assign people to read the parts from the book, as they may take the assignment personally.

> Place: Generic school, USA—the victims' ages can be adjusted to meet the needs of the participants
>
> Time: The present
>
> Motive: To be determined by the group of detectives
>
> Suspects: Everyone

The leader has people draw characters out of a hat or bag, so there can be no accusation of stereotyping.

## Phase I

This first phase should take no more than 15 minutes.

- ◆ Ben and Ima Learner read their biographies to the group. Tessy Temptaker reads her biography and the school nurse's report to the group.
- ◆ Each character reads his or her biography to the group. The characters may repeat information from their biographies, but they may not add any information.
- ◆ The large group is then divided into smaller groups of three. The triad becomes the prosecution, the defense, and the jury.
- ◆ The first task of the triad is to identify two prime suspects and their motive.
- ◆ Next, they are to list which attitudes among those described by the characters are most damaging and why.
- ◆ The group should come to a consensus about the reasons for their choices and present those reasons to the entire group (time limit 10 minutes).

There may be more than one guilty character, but the entire group must agree on that decision.

## Phase II

In this phase, a plan of action is developed (10 minutes).

- ◆ After all of the groups have shared their suspects and motives, the groups reassemble in their original triads.

- The groups are given the following task: At this time, as leaders in your school, you know you must take action to remove DATA from your building. Your task is to make a five-part plan to work on the attitudes of those who kill learning. (At this time, the mystery sides with rehabilitation). Write your plan on newsprint or a blank transparency and be prepared to share it with the other groups.

- Groups share plans of action for eliminating DATA from the school. The plans are combined, and the mystery is solved.

- Each triad generates a list of positive characteristics and attitudes that all teachers should have. Those characteristics are shared with the larger group.

## Phase III

Plans of action are combined into a written document and returned to the participants. Leaders use the suggestions for future planning.

## Tessy Temptaker

Tessy Temptaker is a mirage in most buildings. Because she is the only district school nurse, she can be in each building only half a day. Tessy spent time in hospital nursing, but she went to work in the schools so that she would not have to work nights. Tessy is concerned about the students and tries hard to answer the many questions they bring to her. She spends most of her time distributing medications, checking inoculations, and filling out forms. Even though she is in each building only a short time each day, she knows a great deal about the students.

# Ima Learner

Ima Learner was born three minutes after her twin brother, Ben. Ima's parents were delighted to have two babies to care for, even though it meant changing their busy professional schedules. Ima's mother was a math teacher and her father a gourmet chef who owned his own restaurant.

Ima had a normal, healthy infancy and early childhood. She entered kindergarten after two years of nursery school, already versed in her alphabet and numbers. Ima loved school, her teacher, and learning. She especially loved art projects, singing, and writing her name.

By the second grade, Ima's love of school had begun to decrease, while the amount of things she had to carry home began to increase. By the fourth grade, she had become convinced that if she did one more hour of seatwork, she would just die. Luckily for Ima, her fourth-grade teacher used simulations, projects, art, music, cooperative learning, and lots of hands-on projects.

By the end of the sixth grade, Ima had developed a glazed stare, the ability to parrot everything she had heard in class, the ability to take many tests, and a vision of herself as a cosmetics saleslady with no homework and lots of free makeup. By the seventh grade, school no longer interested Ima, and although the quantity of assignments had increased, the quality of her school life and her work had dwindled to nothing. Because of her attitude and lack of motivation, Ima was sent to the nurse's and counselor's offices. The nurse referred Ima to her family doctor, who referred her to specialists, who issued the school nurse's report to the school.

# Ben A. Learner

Ima's twin brother Ben came into the world as a good-looking and athletic boy. He, too, had the good fortune to be born into a healthy, caring, and successful family. Like his sister, he entered school eager to learn and anxious to please, and he had an uncanny ability to kick, pass, run, and throw. He was immediately placed in the advanced physical education group and played kickball with the third graders when he only a first grader. Ben had no qualms about using his physical energy in class, but his kindergarten teacher understood learning styles and let him work in an unconfined area. By the first grade, his expectation was that everyone would let him do that. Boy, was he surprised when his first-grade teacher tried to make him stay in his seat. Ben learned in the first grade that school was a game to see who had the power to get you to do something. He especially hated the rule that said you had to stand by the wall at recess if your work was not completed. By the end of the fourth grade, he had become a pro at the game of school. He lost interest in learning and concentrated instead on how much he could get away with in class. The more his teachers tried to settle him in, the more he rebelled. He frequently heard teachers comparing him to his quiet, passive sister.

By the end of the sixth grade, Ben had lost interest in anything except gym class and figuring out how to beat the system. Ben A. Learner, too, had become disengaged. Fearing a hereditary disease, his teachers referred Ben to the school nurse as well, and she referred him to a professional.

# School Nurse's Report on Ben and Ima Learner

After referrals to the university hospital staff for extensive probing, poking, and discussion with students Ben and Ima Learner, the professionals have declared that someone has killed their DTL (desire to learn) and that they are the victims of DATA (deadly attitudes and teacher actions). Although they are still functional in out of school activities, they have suffered a total lack of receptivity to the schooling process. Evidence indicates that this receptivity was present in the early grades, but it has been totally wiped out as of grade 7.

Fearing an epidemic of dysfunctional DTL, the entire seventh-grade class was tested during the holiday break. Most of them are suffering the same symptoms, and some even replied "What school?" when asked whether they were anxious to get back after break. They, too, are the victims of DATA.

The examiners believe it may be possible to save many of the students if the DATA is eliminated from the building. We must work together to determine what exactly killed Ben and Ima's desire to learn and rid our school of DATA if we are ever to have a successful seventh grade.

# Penny Principal

Penny Principal is "in charge" of her building. She has worked very hard to develop her authoritarian style and does not let anyone forget that she makes all the decisions. She only believes in self-empowerment and does not even allow teachers to talk at faculty meetings. She runs her building like a military command center, with no interaction between herself and anyone else. She is totally unapproachable to students and staff and gives weekly calendars of items that must be accomplished. All lesson plans are subject to careful scrutiny and criticism. Parents avoid the school as much as possible. She follows every state mandate to the letter and has vowed never to let flexibility to enter her building. She rules by fear and intimidation. After her first year, she began to wonder why the test scores had gone down and why teachers were asking for transfers. She is the perfect example of how to lose support for the administration building. Teachers whisper to each other in the parking lot, "Be careful what you ask for in a leader, you might get it."

## Peter Principal

Peter Principal was hired because he was highly motivated to make a difference. He said all the right things during the interview, knew someone on the board of education, and received rave reviews from his former staff (who were anxious to get rid of him). All of his goals are personal goals. He wants to be a superintendent and would do whatever is necessary to get to the top. His personal motto is, "It doesn't matter who you step on going up the ladder if you don't plan on going back down. " He hasn't had a new idea in 10 years, but there is never any "trouble" in his building. He quickly discourages new ideas among his teachers by saying, "We tried that in my old school and it did not work," "It's just not in the budget to do that," or "We don't want to have to answer any parent questions, do we?"

He is condescending to the teachers and students and spends most of his time on the phone posturing for a higher position in the district. He has maintained the failing status quo in his building, and nothing has changed or improved during his time there.

# Dr. Daily Decree

Dr. Daily Decree had a list of credentials that amazed the school board that hired him. He is a specialist in several content areas, a constant participant in conferences and workshops, and a bandwagon hopper. The only skill he lacks is the ability to work with people. Every week, he decrees some change in his school. He goes off to a conference, gathers some new ideas, and tells his staff to start doing them. His most famous flop was the magic circle. With proper staff development, the magic circle is a great way for students to share ideas and concerns. However, this school leader did not believe staff development was necessary. On Monday morning, he announced that every classroom that day would have a magic circle for 15 minutes. Unfortunately, he failed to tell his teachers what this was, so speculation and frustration were high among the staff members. Some wondered whether it was an assembly, others thought it might have something to do with the lighting, but most just dismissed it as another one of his strange ideas. No one did anything different but most waited to see whether anything would happen in their classrooms.

# Tilly Testalot

Tilly's parents wrote the book on behavioral objectives. Their objective was to have a baby girl that weighed no more than 8 pounds at birth. Tilly, luckily, weighed in at 7 pounds, 9 ounces. Tilly's entire life was run by objectives. In her early years, she frequently heard her mother say, "No, Tilly, the objective of sitting here is to use this potty four times out of five." It is no small wonder that Tilly began to think in behavioral terms herself.

Now, as a teacher, Tilly is a master at measurement. Her seventh graders know that there will be a test every day and an extra makeup test if they are absent or tardy. Her classroom routine never varies, and her students are fast approaching the world record for having taken the most tests in one year.

Because she is so busy testing, Tilly never has time to actually teach. She did, however, volunteer to be on the committee that was in charge of writing the new state achievement tests.

Tilly can tell you the stanine, mean, median, and mode for her entire class. She knows every student by his or her state test score but has a difficult time remembering their names. Tilly keeps the 24 keys to her many file cabinets on a chain. She locks everything and keeps files on everyone. She has never had a discipline problem.

# Sam (or Samantha) Sarcasm

Sam is the most negative of followers. She is sarcastic to her colleagues, leaders, and students. Every idea that is expressed is fodder for her sarcastic remarks and jokes. She monopolizes meetings by causing undue stress among participants. She uses her sarcasm to avoid being chosen for committees and having to change. In the classroom, she takes her daily frustrations out on her students. Students are never given positive feedback because they don't do anything right. Sam talks much but teachers little.

She attends all school improvement meetings with a newspaper to read. Spend 15 minutes with Sam, and you will begin to doubt your own self-worth and the future of the world.

## Noah Substance

Noah was born while his mother was finding herself. She never did, but she never paid much attention to Noah either. Noah received tenure during an interim principal's time in office.

Noah works in the school, but he has no idea what is going on and does not care. He does only what he has to do—no more. He is known only for the colorful posters that have hung on his classroom walls for six years. He has never proposed a new idea, supported an idea, or participated in any changes. He could care less who the leader is because he follows no one—except the voices in his head.

# Steve (or Susie) Specialty

Steve has a double master's degree in learning disabilities and gifted education. He believes that students must be one or the other. Average and normal do not exist in his world. Steve is intense, aggressive, and never wrong. He believes that he truly understands children, knows what is best for them, and has more concern for their potential than an "ordinary" teacher. Steve does not bother with ordinary things like curriculum planning, grading, and teaching. He just pulls kids out of class for "treatments." He never sees more than six students at a time and has convinced himself that he could never be an ordinary teacher. He refuses to team or work with anyone because they simply do not understand him and his program.

## Tota Lee Complacent

Tota Lee couldn't care less what happens in the school. She has no opinion on any issue and wants to be left alone in her classroom, where she does as little teaching as possible. She, too, avoids all faculty discussions, never volunteers, and does the minimum necessary to keep her job. Students are not exactly sure what she is supposed to be doing, but they know she does not care what they do during her class. She has no classroom management skills, but she does not care.

## Ben There and
## His Buddy, Don That

These two have banded together to make sure the status quo is maintained. It does not matter whether it is working for the students. They do not want any changes in the school. As soon as any change is suggested for consideration and study, they stand and deliver a speech that is already familiar to other faculty members. They cite the one time they tried something new and it did not work. They are famous for recalling all of the negative aspects of changes that did take place.

Their comfort level as teachers is threatened by new leadership and change. They assume that they are leaders among the faculty, but they have few followers.

## Willie Fold

Willie has been on the faculty longer than anyone else, and he has been using the same curriculum, tests, and assignments for 30 years. He figures that he can outlast any new idea—that most leaders will give up after trying to get him to change. He thinks of new leadership as a card game in which he holds all the trump cards. After all, he has outlasted six principals. Parents can help their students study for tests because they are the same tests they took as students. Willie wants to retire to a fishing cabin in Michigan, but he has two years to go. He has a calendar on his office wall on which he crosses off the days until he can retire.

## Sara Seesall

Sara Seesall is the school secretary. She knows anything about anyone. She has no qualms about gossiping openly in the school office. She frequently says to students, "I expect that behavior from you because your brother was here last year and he could not accomplish anything either." Sara's public relations skills are nonexistent, but she is the wife of the school board president. The teachers and students are afraid to come to the office for fear of having their business broadcast to everyone. When Sara goes on vacation, the entire building breathes a sigh of relief.

# Melvin (or Molly) Media

Melvin is the king of movies. Melvin is technically qualified to teach social studies because he had a minor in U.S. history in 1965. He has taught for 11 years at the high school but has been transferred to the middle school. He has no idea how to teach history to seventh graders. He has developed a plan to teach everything by film so that he won't have to prepare much. He holds the record at the county media center for the most films ordered in a week, month, and year. His students have asked for a popcorn machine in the room. He has no intention of following the state standards unless the students happen to pick something up in a film. Of course, that would be difficult because they never discuss the films in class.

## Utter Lee Disorganized

Utter Lee is a leader's nightmare. This person is so disorganized and unprepared that they cannot work with a team nor with other colleagues. They lose important information, are personally dysfunctional, and have little sense of the reality of the organization. Their students suffer and they have no ability to work on committees or future plans. They spend their time trying to figure out what they were supposed to have done yesterday. They are not a reluctant follower, they just never found out there was anyone or anything to be followed.

# Epilogue

The success stories offered in this book and the interviews with school leaders include many of the same suggestions for dealing with reluctant followers. The following suggestions appeared in almost all of the interviews:

- Lead by example.
- Listen to reluctant followers first, then talk.
- Determine the degree of the resistance.
- Establish a proactive support group of those who embrace change.
- Use good teachers as a method of passing along information.
- Use representative councils for decision making.
- Be upfront about concerns when people are not following the plan.
- Establish a formal communications system that includes all involved parties—including students, parents, and the community.
- Emphasize that all change is for the purpose of improving student learning.
- Be clear about the purpose of change.
- Use a visioning or long-term planning process for all changes.
- Establish the norms for decision making before the change process begins.
- Give followers the resources they need to make the necessary changes.
- Celebrate the talents and successes of all participants.
- Value the opinions and ideas of all who are involved.

- Be the hardest worker in the group.
- Correctly interpret what others are saying.
- Tell the truth.
- Expect excellence.
- Ask for help if necessary.

# Index